FAVORITE COUNSELING
AND THERAPY TECHNIQUES

FAVORITE COUNSELING AND THERAPY TECHNIQUES

51 Therapists Share
Their Most Creative Strategies

*Includes contributions from Albert Ellis, William Glasser,
Arnold A. Lazarus, Allen E. Ivey, Raymond J. Corsini,
Peter R. Breggin, Judith S. Beck, and other accomplished helpers.*

Howard G. Rosenthal, Ed.D., Editor

ACCELERATED DEVELOPMENT
A member of the Taylor & Francis Group

USA	Publishing Office:	ACCELERATED DEVELOPMENT
		A member of the Taylor & Francis Group
		325 Chestnut Street, Suite 8
		Philadelphia, PA 19106
		Tel: (215) 625-8900
		Fax: (215) 625-2940
	Distribution Center:	ACCELERATED DEVELOPMENT
		A member of the Taylor and Francis Group
		47 Runway Road, Suite G
		Levittown, PA 19057
		Tel: (215) 269-0400
		Fax: (215) 269-0363
UK		Taylor & Francis Ltd.
		4 John Street
		London WC1N 2ET
		Tel: 071 405 2237
		Fax: 071 831 2035

FAVORITE COUNSELING TECHNIQUES: 51 Therapists Share Their Most Creative Strategies

2 3 4 5 6 7 8 9 0   E B E B   9 8 7

This book was set in Times Roman. Technical development by Cynthia Long. Cover design by Michelle Fleitz.

A CIP catalog record for this book is available from the British Library.
∞ The paper in this publication meets the requirements of the ANSI Standard Z39.48-1984 (Permanence of Paper)

Library of Congress Cataloging-in-Publication Data

Favorite counseling and therapy techniques: 51 therapists share their most creative strategies/Howard G. Rosenthal, editor.
    p. cm.
    "Includes contributions from Albert Ellis, William Glasser, Arnold Lazarus, Allen E. Ivey, Raymond Corsini, Peter Breggin, Judy Beck, and other accomplished helpers."
    Includes bibliographical references.

    1. Counseling. 2. Psychotherapy. I. Rosenthal, Howard, 1952–.
BF637.C6F38   1997
158'.3—dc21

                          97-27881
                             CIP

ISBN 1-56032-667-0 (paper)

CONTENTS

ACKNOWLEDGMENTS

Imagine the thrill and excitement of stepping into the offices of some of the finest therapists in the world as they reveal the intricacies of their favorite counseling and therapy techniques. Imagine what you could learn and how you could integrate this knowledge into your own practice to enhance your therapeutic work. Thanks to the present text, you will not have to imagine it—you can, and by all means will be capable of doing it!

First and foremost, I would like to thank each and every therapist who took time out of his or her schedule to contribute to this book. Without the spirit of intellectual and artistic generosity of the therapeutic contributors, this text would not have been possible. Many of the contributors suggested other potential contributors, thus making the arduous task of compiling this book a little easier.

Next accolades go to my wonderful students—Chris Carlson, Farrah Schneider, Sister Cecilia Marie Vasquez, and Kim Narsh—who helped with the nuts and bolts of the operation. The hundreds of hours of work they put into tracking down therapists, finding their books, and mailing them letters, certainly did not go unnoticed. And of course, Joanne Galanis of the St. Louis Community College at Florissant Valley Library, deserves a round of applause for her outstanding research assistance.

My wife, Patricia, a consummate behavioral scientist herself, made numerous suggestions that helped the manuscript really come alive. I also applaud my two sons, three-and-a-half-year-old Paul and six-month-old Patrick, for putting up with my incessant work on the computer. For anyone who wants an appetizer, so to speak, to the main course of psychotherapeutic techniques included herein, try this simple creative visualization strategy: Visualize me perusing and reformatting a manuscript by Ellis, Lazarus, Glasser, or Ivey, holding baby Patrick in my right hand as I am struggling to keyboard with a single finger on my left hand. Patrick—who looks like he crawled out of a Times Square billboard advertisement for baby powder and is unusually easy to entertain—is laughing uncontrollably at me interacting with the computer monitor. All the while, Paul is tugging on my left shoulder with a book sporting a picture of the man in the moon and asks: "What's his last name, Daddy? What's his middle name? How come he's all alone in the sky? What's holding him up there, Daddy?" The present work, I'm sorry to say, will not adequately answer Paul's thought provoking questions!

I also must mention Cynthia Long of Accelerated Development Publishers who has the ability to tweak a manuscript into a finely tuned book. Lastly, I want to personally thank my editor, contributor, and co-author of a previous book, Dr. Joseph Hollis, who has always been so supportive of my ideas. Joe welcomes creativity in psychotherapy, and that, my dear reader, is truly what this book is all about.

Make yourself comfortable. The psychotherapeutic adventure is about to begin!

ALPHABETICAL LIST
OF TECHNIQUES

SERENDIPITOUS SUGGESTION: AN INTRODUCTION TO THE WONDERFUL WORLD OF PSYCHOTHERAPEUTIC TECHNIQUES

"The aberrations of the mind, so I had always thought, were for others. . . .
But now, as I listen from my chair behind the couch I know better. I know
that my chair and the couch are separated only by a thin line. I know that
it is, after all, but a happier combination of accidents that determines, finally,
who shall lie on the couch, and who shall sit behind it."
—Robert Lindner, psychoanalyst and author,
The Fifty Minute Hour (1973), p. 207

His classmates had dubbed him the "Ape Man." To be sure, Marty, a fresh-
man at a local high school, struck a posture more reminiscent of the great apes
than that which is the norm for the species Homo sapiens. Marty spent the
better part of each day staring at the ground, rarely looking a soul in the eye,
and on occasion would grunt when spoken to. Slumped over before me was an
adolescent who embodied nearly every possible symptom that comes to mind
when one mentions the term "inferiority complex." Worse yet, this lad was convinced beyond a shadow of a doubt that he was exceptionally ugly. Because of
this false conviction, Marty—despite the fact that he appeared totally normal

1

and was free of any physical disabilities—walked with his upper torso bent over nearly parallel to the floor.

Though Marty probably never was eligible for any prizes of mental health, his own account (and that of his family) was that his present state of self-proclaimed inferiority escalated dramatically after he experienced an unusually embarrassing moment in front of a large number of his peers. The kids in the neighborhood, and those who attended his high school, would never let him forget it, nor would he afford himself the luxury.

When I met Marty, he informed me that one of his goals was to meet and possibly date a nice young woman. Although it might sound cruel, Marty's personality and overall demeanor convinced me that he had about as much chance of meeting and sustaining a relationship with a nice young lady as I did of winning the lottery that day, and I hadn't even purchased a ticket. Lest the reader get the wrong idea, I must emphasize that I had a wealth of empathy. Unfortunately, it was laced with a lethal dose of therapeutic pessimism.

Although Freud in his wisdom had made great strides with the Wolf Man and the Rat Man, my initial nondirective sessions with this client who the kids unmercifully had nicknamed the "Ape Man" were anything but promising. Again and again I would ask myself what needed to transpire so that Marty could change. Finally it occurred to me that I would need to do something different, something strange—in fact, something downright drastic! And something different, something strange, something drastic, I did.

I enlisted the help of my talented colleague, Amy Hilgemann. (Today Amy is the Executive Director of Behavioral Health Alternatives, Inc., in Wood River, Illinois.) Amy and I met to plot an innovative course of therapeutic action intended to head Marty's self-deprecating tendencies off at the pass. After extensive brainstorming, Amy and I came up with an intervention that could be implemented so swiftly that Marty would barely be aware it of its existence. Like criminals scheming a bank robbery or a jewelry heist, we wanted to get in and get out quickly before Marty could consciously process and possibly negate what had transpired.

During our next session, Marty, per usual, sat bent over staring at the empty desktop that separated our chairs. Without warning, Amy came running into the room yelling, screaming, and flailing her hands in the air. Her verbalizations centered around a client who supposedly severely beat her children.

"Damn it," I yelled, as I pounded my fist on the desk, nearly breaking the surface. My exceptionally loud belligerent comments and my forceful blow on the desktop forced Marty to sit up and take a gander at what was going on in the room. I continued, though very briefly, with my contrived tirade. "Okay," I remarked, "I've had it with that lady. Call the police and have her arrested. I want her kids yanked out of the home. Now!"

As Amy turned around to exit the room, she smiled coyly and said, "Hey, is that your friend? Gosh, he's really cute." Marty looked perplexed. Perhaps dumbfounded would be a more accurate description. Before he could utter a single word, I interjected, "Oh, no big deal, Marty; I'm sure you hear that from women all the time." I then changed the subject intentionally to the topic of his schoolwork.

Although only a knave, a fool, or a neophyte clinician would suggest that Marty was *cured*, I'll have you know that he walked out of the session with a more optimistic attitude, and, for the first time since I had met him, *he was sporting an upright posture.*

I was so enthralled with the power of this technique that I dubbed the strategy "Serendipitous Suggestion" and wrote the results in an article to share my thoughts with other practitioners (Rosenthal, 1983). The physiologist Cannon (1945) had set the groundwork by using the term "serendipity" (from Horace Walpole's fairy tale, *The Three Princes of Serendip*) to depict a research study in which an hypothesis is tested but accidentally reveals an even more valuable discovery. Likewise, I described serendipitous suggestion as a situation in which a client expects one suggestion yet discovers another (often more valuable) suggestion in the process of attempting to perceive the first suggestion.

SIX KEY REASONS WHY TECHNIQUES CAN ENHANCE YOUR THERAPEUTIC EFFECTIVENESS

Based on Marty's progress and the improvement I noticed in numerous other clients using this and a myriad of other strategies, I became sold on the value of techniques. From that time forward, I routinely would scan scholarly works and compare notes with colleagues, searching for innovative techniques that might help when traditional interventions proved ineffective.

Creative interventions infiltrated their way into my therapy sessions. On numerous occasions, for example, I utilized paradoxical strategies urging insomniacs who routinely would awaken at a given hour in the middle of the night to set their alarm clocks to awaken themselves 20 or 30 minutes early. More often than not, these clients who had chased the sandman unsuccessfully and counted more sheep than they cared to remember would turn off the alarm, roll over, and get some sleep.

When I was working in a hospital setting, a woman who had been through endless courses of treatment exclaimed that she had experienced panic attacks every night for six months and challenged me to abate them. "Because of my condition, I haven't slept a wink in ages, and I want to know what in the heck you're going to do about it." I decided to give her a therapeutic assignment for that very evening. I insisted that prior to the onset of her nightly attack she purposely should bring on an attack—more severe than any in the past—so that the nursing staff could monitor her physiological response. "You're crazier than I am, Dr. Rosenthal," she remarked. The next morning she chided me in group therapy: "You're not half as smart as you think, Dr. Rosenthal. I couldn't bring on an attack, and I slept like a baby." (Crazy like a fox, I guess.) Therefore, based on my own therapeutic successes with paradox, serendipitous suggestion, and a host of other methods, I was and still am a fervent proponent of techniques. The following are six key reasons why I am convinced that techniques can improve the efficacy of your counseling and therapy sessions.

1. *A technique often allows the client to surmount an impasse or sticking point.* Certainly it was true in Marty's case.
2. *A technique sometimes renews the client's interest in therapy.* I remember a situation in which I was running therapy groups in a stress unit using primarily a person-centered therapy approach. One day after utilizing a host of techniques I overheard a client in the hall tell another client, "We finally did something different, and I think it really helped a lot of us."
3. *A technique or strategy offers an escape from the humdrum experience of doing the same thing session after session, a practice that, at best, shuns creativity, intimates that the human practitioner can be replaced by computer therapists or perhaps hypnotic cassettes, and leaves the helper and helpee with a frightening case of déjà vu.* In short, techniques add variation and/or creativity to the psychotherapy sessions and thus can help curb burnout on the part of both parties.
4. *A technique can be used as an adjunct to any brand or modality of therapy.* Thus, a person-centered practitioner or a logotherapist can learn a rational-emotive behavior therapy technique, implement it, and then return to his or her psychotherapeutic treatment of choice.
5. *A technique is often the factor that the client insists is responsible for his or her change and remembers as the zenith or high point of*

treatment. When I worked in an inpatient and aftercare chemical dependency unit, we would administer an evaluation to determine what the client felt helped him or her the most. I was amazed—even though I already was convinced that techniques had merit—by the sheer number of clients who accredited a technique or strategy (similar to many of the interventions our experts will share with you in this text) as the primary curative factor. Certainly clients' self-reports such as this are often inaccurate. Still, the large number of clients who mentioned a technique, strategy, or therapeutic exercise made it difficult to dismiss categorically their assessment of what was most valuable.

6. *A technique can be extremely efficacious when applied to a given symptom, difficulty, or disorder.* Systems of psychotherapy and counseling are often applicable to all forms of emotional discord. Many techniques, nevertheless, are much more focused and zero in on a specific client population or issue. This indeed gives them a great deal of psychotherapeutic firepower. Frank Dattilio's SAEB System described in this book is useful for panic attacks, while Edward Beck's Vocation Fantasy Empowerment technique (based on his mentor Robert Hoppock's work) is best suited for clients struggling with career and vocational choice issues. Other techniques herein focus primarily on children, grief, lack of assertive behavior, borderline personality disorder, habit control, couples, families, or group work to name a few.

THE EVOLUTION OF THIS BOOK

On approximately the 15-year anniversary of Marty's upright march from his counseling session, I contacted Accelerated Development publisher and editor, Dr. Joseph Hollis, to discuss the possibility of compiling a volume devoted solely to sharing therapists' favorite techniques. Joe was quite enthusiastic and agreed that the idea definitely had merit.

I began my search with one arbitrary stipulation; namely, that all contributors needed to be the author or co-author of a book in the field. My definition of "a book in the field" was indeed a very loose one: a clinical book, a college text, a psychoeducational workbook for children, or even a popular bibliotherapeutic work for adults would meet the requirement. My hypothesis was that, for the most part, clinicians who met this requirement would possess a higher than average degree of experience as well as the ability to communicate that experience (*ergo,* their favorite technique) to others. Probably more important, however, was the fact that this requirement would keep me from unconsciously, or worse yet consciously, packing the book with responses from friends and colleagues I have met over the years. Thus, by instituting this policy, I felt that fairness would prevail.

Needless to say, there are thousands upon thousands of therapists who have never written a book who possess impeccable credentials, skills, and creativity, and these individuals could no doubt have contributed superb responses. Deciding how to canvas this huge number of therapists, however, was another reason I chose a more specific population (i.e., those who had authored/edited one or more books).

Ultimately, I believe that fairness did prevail. There is only one therapist in our entire cast of characters whom I would consider a personal friend.

Incidentally, the types of books that our contributors have authored are rich in variation. Some of our contributors have written world renown works, classics, or staples in the field. Albert Ellis's *Reason and Emotion in Psychotherapy* (1988), William Glasser's *Reality Therapy* (1965), Arnold Lazarus's *Behavior Therapy and Beyond* (1971), and Raymond Corsini's *Encyclopedia of Psychology* (co-authored with Danny Wedding, 1987) surely would fall into this category. Other contributors authored works that have had a tremendous impact on the popular press such as psychiatrist Jerold Kreisman's book, *I Hate You Don't Leave Me: Understanding the Borderline Personality* (1991), and psychiatrist Peter Breggin's best seller, *Talking Back to Prozac: What Doctors Aren't Telling You about Today's Most Controversial Drugs* (1994). Others have produced noteworthy textbooks. Scott Meier's *Elements of Counseling* (1993) and Ed Neukrug's *Theory, Practice and Trends in Human Services: An Overview of an Emerging Profession* (1994) both are works that I currently utilize in college classes that I teach.

Perhaps the most creatively different work would be social worker Missy Korenblat-Hanin's *The Asthma Adventure Book* (Korenblat-Hanin & Moffet, 1993), published by Fisons, a pharmaceutical firm, which is intended to help children deal with the emotional aspects of their respiratory ailment.

As you read this text, you will note immediately that it includes some of the most accomplished and highly credentialed therapists in the world.

- Psychologist Albert Ellis is the founder of Rational-Emotive Behavior Therapy and has authored over 50 books and monographs as well as over 500 journal articles.
- Psychiatrist William Glasser is the father of Reality Therapy.
- Psychologist Arnold Lazarus created Multimodal Therapy and is considered one of the most influential psychologists of all time.

- Psychiatrist Peter R. Breggin is the National Director for the Center for the Study of Psychiatry and Psychology.
- Psychologist Richard H. Cox is the President of the Forest Institute of Psychology.
- Counselor and psychologist Robert E. Wubbolding is the Director for the Center for Reality Therapy.
- Social worker Robert Taibbi has written over 100 journal and magazine articles.
- Psychologist Allen E. Ivey has written over 20 books and 200 articles/ book chapters, and popularized the concept of microcounseling attending skills applicable to nearly any psychotherapeutic approach.

These are just a few examples. Many of the professionals who contributed are so well credentialed that their complete vitae could rival the size of this entire book. Hence, when you see the heading "Major Works" at the beginning of each therapist's technique, please understand that it could not possibly come close to doing justice to the contributor.

THE TECHNIQUE ACQUISITION PROCESS

When soliciting responses, no attempt was made to give preference to one group of professionals over another (e.g., psychologists over counselors, or social workers over psychiatrists). Nor was it my intent to push one therapeutic modality over another (e.g., behavior therapy over psychodynamic therapy). To acquire the responses in this text was an arduous task. It took several years and literally thousands of letters. The following are the major steps taken in the acquisition process.

1. Letters were mailed to all authors who had published a book with the Accelerated Development division of the Taylor & Francis Publishing Group, because they specialize in psychologically based books and would be producing the present tome.
2. Letters were mailed to authors who created works in the field for other major publishers specializing in counseling, psychology, family therapy, and psychotherapeutic titles. I often asked book representatives from these companies for leads and combed the companies' book catalogs.
3. Letters were mailed to the directors of every Council for the Accreditation of Counseling and Related Educational Programs (CACREP) graduate counseling program in the U.S.

4. Letters were mailed to the director of every American Psychological Association (APA) doctoral clinical psychology program in the U.S.
5. Letters were mailed to every National Association of Social Workers (NASW) graduate school of social work in the U.S.
6. Letters were mailed to every accredited school of psychiatry in the U.S.
7. Letters were mailed to all accredited 29 psychoanalytic training institutes in the U.S.
8. Letters (usually certified with return receipt post cards attached) were sent to numerous major figures in psychology, counseling, social work, psychiatry, family therapy, and psychoanalysis. Tracking these folks down was often quite difficult. I used a number of methods including telephone directories, *The National Register of Health Providers in Psychology,* the *American Counseling Association's 1996 Membership Directory,* the computer disks listing the *1995 Directory of National Certified Counselors,* and current and past copies of the *American Psychological Association's Membership Directory.* I often acquired valuable information from workshop promoters, other professionals who knew the person in question, as well as reference room librarians.
9. Press releases were sent to the American Counseling Association's *Counseling Today,* the American Psychological Association's *Monitor,* and the National Association of Social Workers' *Newsletter.*

My only disappointment was that many of the counselors and therapists whom I contacted graciously turned me down because of numerous projects they were working on themselves. A number of accomplished helpers and pioneers in the field stated that they were retired. Perhaps the most humorous response I received came from a prominent psychiatrist who, after stating that he was retired, shared with me that fly fishing is currently his favorite therapeutic technique.

Figure 1.1 displays a copy of the letter mailed to all therapists, while Figure 1.2 shows the format contributors were asked to follow when composing their contribution. Figure 1.3 is the letter mailed to CACREP, APA, NASW, psychiatry, and analytic directors or program chairpersons. Needless to say, because every therapist needed to have the information contained in the letters, these were included in all packets sent to program directors and chairs. A post-paid envelope was included with every packet mailed. The letter to potential contributors evolved ever so slightly as the project matured; the changes were, at best, minor.

My materials to potential contributors did not discern any differences between the terms *technique* and *strategy.* Rather than splitting theoretical hairs,

Dear Dr.   :

As a well-known authority, **your input** is being solicited for a book I am editing for Accelerated Development/Taylor & Francis Publishers. The book is tentatively entitled *Favorite Counseling and Therapeutic Techniques.* The book is being compiled in response to requests for a list of techniques used by authorities in the profession.

You have been selected based on your professional reputation and/or knowledge in the helping professions. Everyone who receives this letter has authored, or co-authored, a book in the field.

The book is based on the assumption that most counselors and therapists have a favorite technique or strategy that works unusually well for them. Because the technique is helpful, perhaps you would be willing to share your procedures with others. Simply describe your technique in the format outlined on the enclosed sheet. A postpaid addressed envelope is provided for your convenience.

The intent is to include unusually creative, innovative, original, or unique techniques used in counseling and therapy. **Your name and affiliation will appear in the text.**

I am looking forward to seeing your **favorite technique** by September 15, 1996, and hope to see it in a format that will be helpful for students and practitioners in the mental health profession.

Sincerely,

Howard Rosenthal, Ed.D., NCC, CCMHC

Figure 1.1. Letter mailed to all therapists.

BRIEF FORMAT FOR WRITING
YOUR FAVORITE COUNSELING
AND/OR THERAPEUTIC TECHNIQUE

Please draft your response on a typewriter or word processor. Remember to double-space.

1. Your name and highest degree as you would like it to appear in the book (e.g., Joe Smith, Ph.D.).
2. Your profession (e.g., licensed counselor, psychologist, board certified psychiatrist, licensed clinical social worker, etc.).
3. Primary affiliations. No more than two (e.g., University of Ohio and private practice).
4. Major works. You may list up to three books. If you have other works, simply say something such as "and 14 other books."
5. Name of technique or strategy (e.g., Guided Imagery for Depression or Role-playing for Children of Divorce).
6. Population for whom technique is appropriate (e.g., children under five in group therapy, Adult Children of Alcoholics in couples counseling sessions, etc.).
7. **Describe your technique in two or three double-spaced pages or less.** Use step-by-step procedures when appropriate. Try to use easy-to-understand language, avoiding technical jargon whenever possible. If you need to reference or document your idea, please do so using APA manuscript style. If your idea is novel, references may be inappropriate.
8. Give any cautionary notes (e.g., Do not use this technique with suicidal, homicidal, or paranoid clients.) and disclaimers (e.g., This hypnotic strategy seems to work well with clients who wish to quit smoking but is ineffective with those who want to lose weight).
9. As soon as I can, I will contact you to let you know if your idea was indeed selected and when the book will be published. Please give me your address, phone number, and fax number in case clarification is needed regarding your strategy.
10. Please send your favorite counseling and/or therapeutic technique to me in the enclosed postpaid return envelope.

**THANK YOU FOR YOUR TIME, KNOWLEDGE,
ASSISTANCE, AND EXPERTISE!**

Figure 1.2. Format of technique contribution.

Dear Director of Clinical Psychology:

I currently am compiling a text entitled *Favorite Counseling and Therapy Techniques* for Accelerated Development/Taylor & Francis Publishers. The book will feature creative therapeutic strategies.

Enclosed you will find a letter that explains the project as well as a format for writing your technique. I would welcome a contribution from yourself or your faculty members. **The only stipulation is that all contributors must already be the author or co-author of a clinical or self-help book in the field.**

Should you or your staff decide to contribute, a postpaid envelope is included for your convenience.

Sincerely,

Howard Rosenthal, Ed.D., NCC, CCMHC

Figure 1.3. Letter mailed to all program directors and department chairpersons.

the terms were used as if they were synonymous. I wanted creative responses. Many of our contributors insisted that they needed more than three pages to do justice to their intervention and in every case I complied with the request.

What precisely is a technique or strategy? The reader will note immediately that there is seemingly little consensus or consistency in the manner in which our panel of experts views, defines, or describes a technique or strategy.

Some of the techniques/strategies described are so broad that the authors view them as complete systems of counseling, psychotherapy, or treatment. Glasser's reality therapy and choice theory, Phoebe Farris-Dufrene's description of art therapy, Robert Firestone's voice therapy, Fred Neuman's social therapy, and Ellen Walkenstein's technique of nucleus therapy all would fall into this complete systems category. Since such strategies are so vast, descriptions of them included here are necessarily a tad esoteric.

At the other end of the spectrum, many of our contributors supplied specific, step-by-step instructions and verbiage similar to what one might expect to find in a mechanical how-to manual. For example, when Jean Marnocha and Beth Haasl describe their "Memory Collage," they will inform us that in order to duplicate their technique, "pencils and markers, magazines that can be cut up, scissors, and paste or glue" will be necessary. Raymond Corsini, drawing on his 50 years of experience as a counselor and therapist, in his "Turning the Tables on the Client: Making the Client the Counselor," will provide precise directives such as, "Now you say: 'I want you to take my chair and sit down.' Then you wait until the person does just that. Should the person ask why, you refuse to answer the first request."

While some helpers relish the thought of specificity, other therapists find this cookbook approach downright distasteful. Permit me to share the final paragraph of an insightful letter I received from psychiatrist and contributor John E. Poarch.

> I am reluctant to add more because of the implication of what to do and what not to do are contained in my metaphor and I certainly want to avoid any implication of trying to facilitate any idea of therapy by the numbers or by recipe. I think that counselors and therapists searching for such "techniques" should be referred for supervision/consultation, and indeed sometimes therapy, in order to increase their tolerance for ambiguity, doubt, and uncertainty. Such tolerance I consider essential.

When we compare Dr. Poarch's thoughts with some of the therapists who espouse step-by-step instructions, it is clear that one therapist's meat is truly another's poison. Ultimately, it is up to each individual helper to discern precisely which techniques he or she feels comfortable using.

Another key issue is that a number of our contributors readily admit that they are not the originators of the strategies about which they are writing. You also will find that, in accordance with my guidelines, quite a few of the contributions include no references or professional documentation. My intent in allowing this practice was to encourage creativity, perhaps beyond that which one could expect to find in most professional books and journals.

For simplicity and consistency, each technique in this book is described in the following format:

Name of the Technique

Name of the author and relevant degrees or certifications.
Primary affiliation of the author.
Major works of the author, including the titles of up to three books.
Population for whom the technique is appropriate.
Cautionary notes.
Description of the technique.
References, if appropriate.

A CAUTIONARY NOTE
FOR THE CAUTIONARY NOTES

I want to add a word of warning here for those who are students, those who are practitioners undergoing supervision, or those who are new to the field. As mentioned earlier, our contributors generally have years and years of experience teamed up with a wealth of therapeutic credentials. You will find some of the finest therapists in the world within these pages. Because of this, perhaps the most common response to my heading "Cautionary Notes" was "None." As the editor of this text, I must point out that if you fall into any of the aforementioned categories (e.g., you are a student in your first counseling practicum), you should discuss the use of any or all of these techniques with your supervisor before implementing them. Moreover, I urge you to peruse current state licensing ethics as well as those set forth by your profession (e.g., ACA, NBCC, NASW, APA, etc.) prior to their usage.

Take the case of Marty recounted at the beginning of this section. Although my colleague, Amy, worked at the same agency I did at the time, it seems evident that in light of today's ethics stressing informed consent, she clearly would need to be defined in the beginning of treatment as a co-therapist. In addition, her beneficial remark to Marty (i.e., "Hey, is that your friend? Gosh, he's really cute.") today would be classified as sexist, *ergo* unethical! Thus, what worked many years ago would in this day and age be deemed an ethical violation. If I were handling the case today, I surely would search for an imaginative course of action, though I would take precautions to assure that my treatment was molded in accordance with contemporary legal and ethical guidelines. You always should strive to do likewise.

Research indicates that empathy is the most predictive indicator of counselor effectiveness (Lafferty, Beutler, & Crago, 1991); hence, practitioners reading this text are advised to display accurate empathy regardless of which technique is being implemented.

Lastly, although this book is decidedly pro-technique, even I must admit that techniques have their pitfalls. Plenty of them. Remember the old medical adage: First do no harm. Indeed techniques have their dark side. I would be remiss if I did not mention them. You will find the whole story in the next section.

Enjoy the rest of the book.

Dr. Howard Rosenthal
St. Louis, Missouri
February, 1997

REFERENCES

Breggin, P. (1994). *Talking back to Prozac: What doctors aren't telling you about today's most controversial drugs.* New York: St. Martin's Press.

Cannon, J. B. (1945). *The way of an investigator.* New York: Norton.

Corsini, R. J., & Wedding, D. (1987). *Encyclopedia of psychology.* Canada: John Wiley and Sons.

Ellis, A. (1988). *Reason and emotion in psychotherapy.* New York: Carol Publishing Group.

Glasser, W. (1965). *Reality therapy.* New York: HarperCollins.

Korenblat-Hanin, M., & Moffet, M. (1993). *The asthma adventure book.* Rochester, NY: Fisons.

Kreisman, J. J. (1991). *I hate you don't leave me: Understanding the borderline personality.* New York: Avon.

Lafferty, P., Beutler, L. E., & Crago, M. (1991). Differences between more and less effective psychotherapists: A study of select therapist variables. *Journal of Consulting and Clinical Psychology, 57,* 76-80.

Lazarus, A. A. (1971). *Behavior therapy and beyond.* New York: McGraw Hill.

Lindner, R. (1973). *The fifty minute hour.* New York: Bantam.

Meier, S. (1993). *Elements of counseling.* Pacific Grove, CA: Brooks/Cole.

Neukrug, E. S. (1994). *Theory, practice and trends in human services: An overview of an emerging profession.* Pacific Grove, CA: Brooks/Cole.

Rosenthal, H. G. (1983). Serendipitous Suggestion in Hypnosis and Psychotherapy. *Hypnosis Quarterly, 25*(2), 22-25.

Part II

THE DARK SIDE OF TECHNIQUES: BEWARE OF THE MILTON H. ERICKSON CLONE

"In the report card of life, nobody gets a mark for effort."
—Andrew Salter, The Father of Conditioned Reflex Therapy

It was a strange twist of fate that a visit to an all-night book store late one evening in 1976 would forever change the way I performed psychotherapy, though hardly in the direction I originally anticipated. While perusing the psychology section, I came across and purchased Jay Haley's 1973 edition of *Uncommon Therapy: The Psychiatric Techniques of Milton H. Erickson, M.D.*

I could sleep hardly a wink that evening, not due to insomnia but rather to the compulsion to flip the page to see what gems of wisdom I would discover next. I marveled as Erickson's psychotherapeutic genius manifested itself again and again on page after page in the text. To be sure, Erickson was doing something new, something different, and best of all something exciting.

Erickson went from one clinical case to another often "curing" seemingly incurable clients of what ailed them in a very short period of time. Even more remarkable was the fact that some of these clients already had undergone traditional therapy with few, if any, results.

I hardly could contain my enthusiasm. I knew that I had discovered a quicker, more efficacious form of treatment, and I was hell-bent on using it. I spent the rest of the day reading files of the clients in my private practice looking for the perfect subject. I needed someone who seemed *similar* to one of Erickson's clients in the book. Finally, I found the ideal person.

I had seen Tom, an eighth-grader at a local school, for five or six sessions, and, according to his mother, he was making sufficient progress. Moreover, Tom had been to a string of therapists, counselors, and caseworkers prior to me and had informed his mother that he liked me the best. Up until this point in time, I had been using a non-directive, person-centered approach, but now I was ready to get out the heavy artillery and bring Erickson into the therapy room with me. A sense of power flowed in my veins. Although Tom's sessions were going well, they were now going to kick into passing gear. Milton Erickson was in my court now. What more could any red-blooded therapist ask for?

Now when I say that I planned to *bring Erickson into the therapy room with me,* I meant it quite literally. My strategy seemed foolproof. Tom's chubby physique caused him ongoing ridicule from his fellow students, and from what I could ascertain it was taking a huge toll on his self-image. I purposely had picked Tom as my subject because in the book Erickson had an obese patient with *similar* characteristics. Erickson was quite blunt with his patient (perhaps downright mean and sarcastic would be more accurate). Since I wanted to be sure I was a perfect Ericksonian clone, I sat behind my desk and positioned Haley's tome on Erickson such that I could read it verbatim yet the client would be unaware of its existence. It seemed like a stroke of genius, though to be sure I felt a little like a youngster cheating on a final exam. I was like a card shark who knew he was playing with a stacked deck and loving every minute of it.

After asking Tom a fairly innocuous question about how his week was going, I began reading Erickson's therapeutic tirade. Since I had committed most of it to memory, I could tell that Tom did not have the foggiest notion that I had a crib sheet (i.e., Haley's book on Erickson).

I had verbalized only the first seven or eight sentences when a strange thing transpired. Instead of the client responding in a positive manner, Tom's eyes rapidly swelled with tears. I had no intention of putting a halt to my plan of action. It worked eloquently for Dr. Erickson, and I was certain it would work for me. In the minutes that followed, Tom was sobbing. The next thing I knew, Tom was bolting out of the office, down the stairs, and out the front door of the building. I never heard from Tom again.

I was spellbound by Tom's puzzling reaction. Didn't he know he was being counseled by the great Milton Erickson? Didn't he know he was supposed to be miraculously cured and lose weight?

After pondering the case for several days, I came to the simple conclusion that Tom was a rare bird and that 99 out of 100 patients in his shoes would have responded favorably to the intervention. Although I didn't know it then, I had learned nothing from the case and was determined to try my Ericksonian clone experiment again in the near future.

Within six months, I was convinced that I had the therapeutic armamentarium I needed. I had acquired an audio tape of Erickson hypnotizing a middle-age gentleman for stress. Erickson's client's difficulties appeared *strikingly similar* to a client I was seeing at the time.

My modus operandi would be the same as before except that I first transcribed Erickson's induction and suggestions on paper so that I could read them. My notes included relevant silences and vocal inflections.

Although this session was not replete with the fireworks displayed in Tom's session (thank god for small favors!), the end result only could be described as disappointing. After the session, my client (unprovoked by me) stated that although the session was not overwhelmingly negative, he *liked the hypnotic style I had used in the past much better, and he asked if I would return to it during future sessions.*

What in the heck was going on here? I gave the client a therapeutic strip steak, and he was pleading for a measly fast-food therapeutic hamburger. How in the world could he request my paltry intervention when he could plug into Erickson's? Well, how could he? This was too much to fathom. I would have to give it some serious thought, but in the interim I decided for the sake of my clients, not to mention my practice, not to conduct anymore Ericksonian clone experiments.

I drew a blank as to what had transpired until sometime later when I was confronted with a 13-year-old female who suffered from Trichotillomania, a condition in which the client pulls out his or her own hair and then generally eats it. My client, Gloria, was described by her mother as "unusually perceptive" and "brilliant."

Since I had sworn off Ericksonian techniques temporarily, I began the interview using a strict, non-directive paradigm. With the exception of the aforementioned Ericksonian disasters, I always seemed to have the ability to judge accurately how well my sessions were progressing. During my initial session with Gloria, I felt I was hitting all the right keys on the Carkhuff empathy scale. The faculty at my graduate school would have been proud. About five minutes into our session, however, Gloria indicated that the treatment was going nowhere fast. In fact, it was going nowhere period.

Said Gloria: "You know. Every time I say something, well, you kind of repeat it in your own words and you seem to do a great job of understanding what I feel. And you're very kind, sincere, and caring. But this isn't all there is to counseling, is it? I mean, we both know you are going to have to do something different to help me stop pulling my hair."

It was at that moment that I learned what it really meant to be an effective therapist. I acquiesced with Gloria and explained that reflection and paraphrasing were used simply for the first few minutes, and then we would swing into action. I ended up successfully treating Gloria with behavioral techniques such as charting and positive reinforcement. In a very short period of time, Gloria was relieved of her *dis-tressing* habit.

The moment I switched strategies with Gloria, I had the "aha" experience of insight I sorely needed to put this situation as well as the Erickson fiascos into perspective.

First, let me assure you that my armchair Ericksonian experiments and the description of Gloria's treatment did not suggest in any way, shape, or form that behaviorism is superior to non-directive methods. Nor did my experience debase the highly creative and superb interventions executed by Erickson and his followers. Instead, these experiences provided me with seven axioms for efficacious treatment that can help any therapist regardless of his or her theoretical persuasion.

1. When you read textbooks written by world famous therapists, keep in mind that they are almost always top-heavy in terms of focusing on successes rather than failures. Even master therapists do not succeed with every client.

2. Do not try to become a clone of Milton Erickson, Carl Whitaker, Carl Rogers, Fritz Perls, or anyone else. It is perfectly natural and even desirable to use their strategies, but be absolutely certain that you bend, fold, mutilate, and alter them to match your comfort level and personality as well as that of your client's. *If you do not feel comfortable with*

a strategy including any of the ones provided in this book, then do not use it. Moreover, if your sessions are going reasonably well as mine were with Tom, then resist the temptation to mimic a famous therapist's strategy. For downright simplicity remember: If it ain't broke, don't fix it!

3. Use extreme caution when you come across a client treated by a well-known therapist who at first glance seems *similar* to a client you are treating. In the case of Tom, I was shocked when Erickson's dialogue backfired. Never mind that upon closer inspection Erickson's client was a female whereas mine was a male. Never mind that Erickson's patient was 21 whereas I was treating an eighth-grader. Never mind that Erickson was seeing his client for the first time whereas I had seen mine for a number of sessions. In retrospect I can only say: What similarities?

   In the case where I used Erickson's hypnotic induction for the middle-age man with stress, I had no knowledge whatsoever about Erickson's client except that he too was under a great deal of stress. My assumption (i.e., that my client was similar to his) probably was just that—an assumption. Do not stereotype your clients.

   The cold, hard truth is that Erickson—precisely because of his creativity and his tendency to treat each client in an individualized, calculated manner—*never* would have utilized the treatment dialogue or hypnotic induction of his that I used to treat either of my clients. He treated each client as a unique individual, and so should you.

4. Just because you are not a world renowned therapist, do not sell yourself short. It is quite possible, for example, that my hypnotic interventions with my stressed out client were indeed more efficient than those of an Ericksonian nature. The grass is not always greener in another therapist's office.

5. If a strategy is not working, do not feel compelled to use it merely because you are a Freudian, a behaviorist, a brief strategic family therapist, or a follower of Milton Erickson. And certainly do not wait until your client runs out of the interview as mine did to decide that it is not succeeding. As noted in my session with Gloria, you often will need to switch gears and institute a new therapeutic ploy at a moment's notice.

6. Realize that what worked with your nine o'clock client probably will not work as well with the one you are seeing at ten, and it even could

fall flat on its face with your eleven o'clock appointment. In fact, that strategy from heaven that worked so well with your nine o'clock client indeed could become the strategy from hell during next week's session with the same client.

7. Accept the fact that there are instances when techniques or canned strategies are not appropriate. For example, when I work with survivors of suicide (i.e., clients who are grieving because someone they knew committed suicide), I can not imagine any contrived technique that would be helpful during the initial moments of the first session—unless, of course, you consider listening intently and providing intense empathy to be techniques.

I also must mention that some experts in our field are vehemently opposed to the use of techniques under any circumstances. One well-known therapist whom I invited to contribute to this book sent my solicitation letter back to me and wrote at the top: "I'm a person-centered therapist. I don't do techniques."

When I asked Jeffrey A. Kottler, Professor of Counseling and Educational Psychology at the University of Nevada, Las Vegas, and the author of 18 books to contribute, he wrote me the following short note:

Dear Howard,

This is certainly not what you wanted but it's the best I can do.

My best,

Jeffrey Kottler

Dr. Kottler enclosed a very insightful piece entitled "Non-techniques" that I shall share here in its entirety.

I do not believe in techniques. I resist the very idea of techniques, that is, the notion that there are particular things we can do for people that will make a difference. For me, counseling is about listening and observing carefully, connecting with clients in a way that they feel understood, and then helping them develop alternative ways of living their lives or at least thinking and feeling differently about their lives. These things that I do are not techniques; rather they are individually designed strategies that reflect the culture, background, values, and goals of each client.

I realize that I am a lone voice in a book such as this that is chock full of things counselors can do. I am also more than a little sympathetic to the feelings of ineptitude that many of us feel that we do not know enough and can not do enough to help those who come to us in such pain and disorientation. I have made a whole career about talking about these fears of failure and about disclosing my own feelings of being a fraud because so much of the time I do not really feel like I know what I am doing.

I have tried to soothe my conscience and appease my fears by attending workshops and buying books such as this that promise the kinds of concrete ideas that I have been so hungry for. If only I could just add another tool to my bag of tricks . . . If only I could discover just one more technique that might help me unlock the secrets of a resistant client's lost soul, to help that person find some sort of peace.

Yet techniques have never done it for me. Never have, never will.

In my hunger to become a better counselor, to become more consistent and effective in my helping efforts, I have found that what I need most is the inner clarity to see and hear what clients are really saying, and then to create some way to reach them so they will treat themselves and others more respectfully, to take the risks that are necessary in order to function more effectively in their lives. I will not find these techniques in a book or a workshop but deep within myself and the unique relationship I have co-created with a client.

Yet what reading about other people's favorite techniques does for me is help me to realize how important it is to stop imitating others who claim to have found "The Way." I start to feel inadequate because I am not smart enough or clever enough to have invented these ideas myself. Then I feel inspired by the creativity of my colleagues. I internalize the process that underlies their thinking about how change often takes place.

I am searching for ways to reach people. I do not do that with techniques but with non-techniques. When I have been able to incorporate the ideas of others into a way of relating to clients that is both compassionate and powerful, that is part of me rather than a method that belongs to someone else, then I am more successful in my helping efforts.

My problem is never that I have a shortage of techniques but rather that I have too many. The hardest part for me is figuring out what to do, when to do it, and how far to push. I therefore would urge the reader to worry less about the technique you select and more about the ways you use yourself to make a difference in other people's lives.

I would like to suggest to the reader that the very name of a column Dr. Kottler edits for *Counseling Today,* "Finding Your Way," provides us with the best advice. Some of us will follow *ways* that include techniques, whereas others never will travel in comfort on this path. I admonish you to choose a path that is compatible with your therapeutic belief system and harmonious with your style of counseling and psychotherapy.

Unfortunately, the genius of another therapeutic master cannot always be transplanted or spliced into the therapy session of your choice. Despite our therapeutic talent, most of us never will match Milton H. Erickson's uncanny creativity. Just getting closer than you were when you started in this profession is enough for most of us. And for those us who do dabble in the art and science of psychotherapeutic techniques, the seven principles listed in this section, combined with the ingenious strategies outlined by the therapists in the pages that follow, are a fine way of doing that.

REFERENCE

Haley, J. (1973). *Uncommon therapy: The psychiatric techniques of Milton H. Erickson, M.D.* New York: Ballantine Books.

Note: An abbreviated version of this chapter appeared in the June, 1996, issue of the American Counseling Association's newsletter, *Counseling Today,* and those portions are reprinted with the permission of ACA.

TECHNIQUES

SYSTEMS-CENTERED THERAPY
FOR GROUPS AND INDIVIDUALS

Therapist: Yvonne M. Agazarian, Ed.D.

Affiliation: Psychologist, Friends Hospital; private practice, Philadelphia, Pennsylvania.

Major works:
> Agazarian, Y. M. (1994). The phases of development and the systems-centered group. In M. Pines & V. Schermer (Eds.), *Ring of fire: Primitive object relations and affect in group psychotherapy.* London: Routledge, Chapman & Hall.
>
> Agazarian, Y. M., & Janoff, S. (1993). Systems theory and small groups. In I. Kapplan & B. Sadock (Eds.), *Comprehensive textbook of group psychotherapy* (3rd ed.). Baltimore, MD: Williams & Wilkins, Division of Waverly.
>
> Agazarian, Y. M., & Peters, R. (1981). *The visible and invisible group: Two perspectives on group psychotherapy and group process.* London: Routledge & Kegan Paul, Ltd. (Reprinted in paperback, 1985.)
>
> Author of 19 other publications.

Population for whom the technique is appropriate: Tailored to goals of change context for populations in mental health and the private and public sectors.

Cautionary notes: None.

25

Defense Modification in Systems-Centered Therapy(™)

Systems-centered therapy is developed from a theory of living human systems and tests the hypothesis that, if the restraining forces to change are modified in a systematic sequence, then driving forces toward therapeutic change will be released. Restraining forces are systematically weakened by modifying defenses in a structured sequence of choices that are within the patient's ability. With each modification, the patient acquires skills that build upon those acquired before and prepare the patient for those that follow. Specific techniques have been developed for each specific modification. Each modification skill acquired meets the goals of a specific therapeutic change assessed by specific outcome criteria. Therapy, therefore, either can be delivered continuously or chunked into modules.

The Hierarchy of Defense Modification

The Social Defenses. Avoidance of unpredictable interpersonal reality by defense, stereotype, or social communications.

The Triad of Symptomatic Defenses.

1. Cognitive distortions: anxiety generated maps of reality, based on negative predictions, speculations, worries, and other defenses against sitting at the edge of the unknown.
2. Tension: avoidance of arousal and emotion by tension, generating stress related, psychosomatic defenses.
3. The retaliatory impulse: avoidance of the retaliatory impulse by depression or hostile acting out of the retaliatory impulse in targeted or random discharges of irritability, frustration and temper.

Role Locks Defenses. Defensive projections and projective identifications into one-up/one-down role relationships such as the following: identified patient and helper; scapegoat and scapegoater; victim and bully; and other defiant or compliant splits that repeat roles from the past.

Resistance to Change Defenses.

1. Externalizing conflicts with authority: defensive stubbornness and suspicion that splits good and bad, and, from a righteous, complaining, and blaming position, externalizes the bad onto authorities or society.
2. Disowning authority: defensive stubbornness and suspicion of self that attributes difficulties in the change process to personal inadequacy rather than reality.

Defenses against Separation and Individuation.

1. Defenses against separation: enchantment and blind trust in others, self, and groups. Merging, symbiosis, and love addiction as a defense against separation.
2. Defenses against individuation: alienation and despair, disenchantment and blind mistrust of self, others, and groups.

Defenses against Knowledge and Common Sense.

1. Defenses against inner reality: defenses against comprehensive and apprehensive knowledge. Being self-centered rather than systems-centered.
2. Defenses against outer reality: defenses against reality testing in the context of the present realities of the role, the goals and the environment. Being self-centered rather than systems-centered.

Technique: Identifying the Source of Anxiety—The Three Questions

Anxiety always is reduced before tackling the turbulence that is present at every boundary crossing. When we are anxious, we tend to see the world through anxious eyes and to make negative predictions that generate still more anxiety. It then becomes difficult, if not impossible, to differentiate between the feelings that are generated by anxiety arising from cognitive distortions and the feelings that are generated by the experiences in reality.

Cognitive Distortions basically bind anxiety by constructing a secondary, alternative reality that reduces the dissonance between the inner and outer world. Secondary realities are created through negative predictions, mind-reading, and externalization. A powerful tool for undoing the anxiety aroused by the turbulence at every boundary are the three questions. Members come to recognize with relative ease that when they are frightened of an unknown reality in the here and now, instead of discovering reality they retreat into explanations or look-alike memories in the past. This binds their fear. Unfortunately, this misconstructed reality generates feelings that *are* real but that signal responses to a world that is *not* real.

1. **Are you thinking something that is making you anxious?** If yes, check for negative predictions or a mind-read.
2. **Do you have a feeling or sensation that is making you anxious?** If yes, introduce the idea of tension as a straightjacket that prevents one from opening up to one's full experience.

3. **Are you anxious because you do not know what is going to happen next?** If yes, introduce the reality that everyone is apprehensive at the edge of the unknown, and it helps to be curious as well.

1. Are You Thinking Something That Is Making You Anxious? Steps to undoing negative predictions and mind-reading are as follows:

*   **Connect the anxiety with the thought:** "Are you telling yourself something that is making you anxious?"
*   **State the thought:** "What are you telling yourself."
*   **Label it as a negative prediction or a mind-read:** "That is a defense called a negative prediction." or "That is a defense called mind-reading." (An "if only" or an "I wish I had" or an "I should have" or "I ought to," etc. are all entrances into constructed reality. It is best, if possible, to train on negative predictions and mind-reading.)
*   **Ask how the patient feels when he or she has that thought:** "How do you feel when you think that?"
*   **Make the connection between the feeling and the thought:** "Do you see then that it is your thoughts that are giving you your feelings?"
*   **Ask whether or not the person believes the thought:** "Do you believe you can predict the future?" or "Do you believe that you can read people's minds?" (If the person believes it, set up a dialogue that results in checking the thought in reality, similar to the undoing of mind-reading.)
*   **Repeat and reframe the experience:** "So you see, you felt anxious and you found that you were making a negative prediction that was making you anxious. You also found out that you felt awful when you were making that negative prediction. Then, when you were asked whether or not you believed it, you found that you didn't. So do you see that you were feeling both awful and anxious about a thought that you didn't believe when you brought it into the light of reality? Do you think that the next time you get anxious you can see if you are having a thought that is making you anxious and see if bringing it into the light of reality makes you feel better?"
*   **Ask what internal reality the person defended against:** "Now you see that your anxiety came from your defenses? Defenses defend against something. Do you know what your experience was in reality that you defended yourself against?" (At this stage in therapy, this is education, as the person may not know himself or herself well enough to answer.)
*   **Introduce the idea that there is a difference between the defensive self and the authentic self:** "We will continue to work so that you can experience the difference between your defensive self, which generates

anxiety and symptoms, and your non-defensive self. You are not yet able to allow yourself to have the true experience of your conflicts and impulses, and as you learn to accept your authentic human responses, you will defend yourself less."

2. Do You Have a Feeling or Sensation That Is Making You Anxious? Steps in undoing anxiety about feelings or sensations are as follows:

- If yes, ask the person to describe the feeling. Ask the person if he or she can make enough space to have the feeling fully.
- If yes, ask the person to explore the experience as he or she discovers it, undoing any cognitive distortions along the way.
- If no, introduce the idea that tension is a straightjacket that prevents one from opening up to the feeling self. Ask the person to pay attention to the feeling inside the tension and explore the experience as it unfolds, undoing any cognitive distortions along the way.
- Repeat the education about defense defending against the authentic self.

3. Are You Anxious Because You Do Not Know What Is Going to Happen Next? Steps to arousing curiosity at the edge of the unknown are as follows:

- If yes, introduce the idea that the person is sitting at the edge of the unknown, and normalize the anxiety by introducing the reality that "everyone is apprehensive at the edge of the unknown."
- Ask if the person is curious about what is going to happen next.
- State that it helps to take your curiosity with you into the unknown.

Driving and Restraining Forces in Relationship to Anxiety

Driving Forces	Restraining Forces
Describe the physical experience of anxiety→	←Escalate anxiety with panicky thoughts, feelings, hyperventilation, faintness, etc.
Ask yourself if you are telling yourself something that is making you anxious. Undo constructed reality by common sense and reality testing→	←Focus on anxiety provoking thoughts that generate distress and still more anxiety: worrying, making negative predictions, mind-reading, etc.
Ask if you are beginning to experience a sensation or feeling that you do not want to feel fully that is making you anxious. Match the thoughts about your feeling with the reality experience of your feeling→	←Believe that to feel is to act, that feelings are overwhelming, dangerous, and drive you crazy without checking the assumptions about feeling with the feeling itself.
Ask if being at the edge of the unknown is making you anxious. Remind yourself to be curious→	←Stereotyping, attacking difference, ignoring, or controlling change, etc.

RESOLVING GRIEF

Therapist: Steve Andreas, M.A.

Profession: Neuro-Linguistic Programming (NLP) trainer; editor/publisher.

Affiliation: NLP Comprehensive, Boulder, Colorado.

Major works:
Andreas, S. (1991). *Virginia Satir: The patterns of her magic.* Mountain View, CA: Science and Behavior Books.
Andreas, S., & Andreas, C. (1987). *Change your mind and keep the change.* Moab UT: Real People Press.
Andreas, S., & Andreas, C. (1989). *Heart of the mind.* Moab, UT: Real People Press.
Has produced over 25 videotaped and audio taped demonstrations of NLP methods.

Cautionary notes: See last paragraph of this article.

Since everyone experiences significant losses if they live long enough, a method for rapidly dealing with the grief response is useful for a wide variety of clients of all ages. Many clients may not recognize a link between unresolved grief and their current difficulties.

To understand the underlying basis of the grief resolution method that my wife, Connirae, and I developed about 10 years ago, think of someone who is very special to you but who is not physically near you at the moment, and notice how you picture that person in your mind.

When I do this with my wife, who is in town on errands, she is standing by my left side, life-size and breathing, and she *feels* present with me, almost as if she were actually in the room. The good feelings that I have had with her are readily available to me, and we call this an *associated* experience. This is only one of many ways to represent an absent loved one, but all of them will result in a sense of the loved one's *felt presence.*

In contrast, someone who is grieving always pictures the lost person as distant or absent in some way. When the client thinks of the person in this dissociated way, he or she cannot experience the good feelings previously enjoyed, resulting in a sense of emptiness and loss. The specific way that a client represents the lost person as absent varies enormously from person to person. The lost person may be seen as a ghostly image, as a dent in the bed but no one is there, or as if the person were on TV, etc.

It is important to realize that these two ways of mentally representing a loved person are independent of "reality." Someone who experiences separation anxiety is representing the person as absent even though the relationship still exists. And those who have grieved successfully represent the loved person as present even though the relationship is over.

A common mistake clients make is to picture the lost love in the throes of terminal cancer or in the last heated argument just before the breakup. This is not the precious experience for which the person is grieving, and it gets in the way of recovering the special feelings that the client had with the lost person.

The first step in resolving grief is to find out how the client represents a person in "felt presence." To discover this, we ask the client to think of (a) a loved person who is not physically present, as described earlier; or better yet (b) a person who is dead or no longer in the client's life, yet when the client thinks of this person, it is with a presently-felt sense of the love, comfort, etc. that the client experienced at the time the valued relationship actually occurred. Exactly how someone visualizes this kind of experience will vary considerably from one client to another, so it is important to find out how *this* particular client does it. This information then will be used as an individual "template" to transform the grief experience into one of felt presence in which the person can enjoy the good feelings of the lost relationship as if it still were occurring.

Next we find out how the client represents the lost person who is the object of grief and loss. The first question is whether the client thinks of the loved one at a time when all the wonderful qualities of the relationship were present. If, instead, the client thinks of the loved one near death or in the argument that ended the relationship, we say "Look, this is not what you miss; what you miss are the special qualities of the relationship you had with this person—the love, comfort, stability, tenderness, humor, spontaneity, or whatever was very special to you about the experiences you shared with that person. Instead of thinking about the end of the relationship, I want you to think of a special time when things were particularly good between you."

Changing the content of the image in this way often temporarily increases the feeling of loss, because the image is still one that is separate or *dissociated* from the client in some way. It is important to proceed directly to using the template of felt presence as a guide to transforming this experience into an *associated* image from which the client can reexperience the good feelings. Often this involves making the image larger or closer, changing it from a dead, still picture into a living movie, stepping into the movie, etc.—whatever is indicated by the template experience of this particular client. When the client reassociates into this experience, there are often tears; they are not tears of loss, but tears of *reunion,* and they typically do not last long.

The relief that people experience through this process is immediate and lasting, and it is a far cry from the acceptance or resignation for which so many people settle. By reuniting with the lost experience, the client regains access to all the special feelings he or she had with that person and continues to carry these resourceful feelings into future relationships. As one client who had been grieving for a lost infant for over six months said a week after a session: "I am flying high!"

There are many other applications of this method that only can be mentioned briefly here. It can be used for any mid-life crisis, when a cherished dream of success, a child, or whatever is lost. Even though the client never actually had the content of the dream in reality, it was so real in the mind that the realization that it will not occur can provoke severe grief. It also can be used for abused clients who are grieving for a loving and secure childhood that they never experienced. "Pre-grieving" can release an ongoing relationship from the dependence and clinging behavior that is based on the fear of future loss. The method also can be used for separation anxiety and for other kinds of losses: things, activities, and location. For some people, the loss of a cherished ring, the loss of the ability to play a life-long sport, or the loss of a family home can be as severe as the loss of a loved person.

Although the brief sketch of the method presented here is enough to work for many clients, there are many specific situations for which a broader understanding of NLP methods are required. For instance, if the death was traumatic, the phobia/trauma cure (Andreas & Andreas, 1989, chapter 7) first must be used with this incident before resolving the grief. If the client has significant anger or resentment toward the lost person, it will be necessary to first help the client reach forgiveness. For further details about these methods, see Andreas and Andreas (1989, chapter 11); for further information about the basic NLP approach, see Andreas and Andreas (1987).

References

Andreas, S., & Andreas, C. (1987). *Change your mind and keep the change.* Moab, UT: Real People Press.

Andreas, S., & Andreas, C. (1989). *Heart of the mind.* Moab, UT: Real People Press.

VOCATIONAL FANTASY:
AN EMPOWERING TECHNIQUE

Therapists: Edward S. Beck, Ed.D., CCMHC, NCC, in honor of Robert Hoppock, Ph.D. (deceased). *Dr. Hoppock died in August, 1995, at the age of 93. He was the author of over 300 articles and was Dr. Beck's advisor and mentor at New York University beginning in 1968. Dr. Hoppock developed the theory and principles of this technique in class. Dr. Beck developed the technique integrating the theory.*

Affiliation: Edward Beck is a professional counselor and Director of the Susquehanna Institute in Harrisburg, Pennsylvania. Robert Hoppock is recognized as a pioneer in the area of vocational counseling and was Professor Emeritus and Chair of Counselor Education at New York University.

Major works:
> Beck, E. S., Seiler, G., & Books, D. K., Jr. (1987). *Training standards for mental health counseling.* Alexandria, VA: American Mental Health Counselors Association.
> Author of over 20 articles on standards, ethics, and professional affairs
> Former Associate Editor, *Journal of Mental Health Counseling.*
> Hoppock, R. (1966). *Occupational information: Where to get it and how to use it.* New York: McGraw-Hill.
> Hoppock, R. (1949). *Group guidance: Principles, techniques, and evaluation.* New York: McGraw-Hill.
> Hoppock, R. (1935). *Job satisfaction.* New York: Harper.

Population for whom the technique is appropriate: This technique is designed for adolescent, young adult, and adult, as well as elderly populations considering vocational choices at all stages of career development (entry level, career changing, etc.).

Cautionary notes: None.

This technique is designed to assess preliminarily a person's underlying vocational aspirations and determine what perceived or real problems may be interfering with reaching those aspirations. The technique also can and should be used as a screening device to see if a formal assessment is absolutely necessary, saving time and costs. The theory underlying this technique holds that a person may genuinely know what job functions, environments, careers, or jobs he or she wants but may not have the necessary information or empowerment strategies to realize the goals. Also, because a person's career aspirations and development may be influenced very strongly by concerns such as self-esteem, self-worth, and other problems, this technique can provide insight as to what mental health problems may be interfering with the aspirations and how they might be relieved with mental health counseling.

Frequently, the fantasy is quite compatible with academic training, prior experience, and career goals. Often, providing occupational information, research strategies, and fine tuning with respect to retraining or curricular adjustment may be indicated, but the client may feel insecure or disempowered to make changes because of a lack of empowering knowledge. Sometimes mental health counseling to relieve distortions and feelings of disempowerment is indicated. The satisfaction derived by both client and counselor using this technique often helps clients reach life-long ambitions, previously thought unattainable.

When the counselor is ready to introduce assessment techniques (testing, computer-assisted programming evaluation, or other), the counselor should offer the following:

> "Before we discuss ways to formally assess your vocational interests, personality, aptitudes, and skills, I'd like to ask you about the following fantasy.
> Just suppose I was an employer, and I told you that I like you and you already have a job with me for more money, security, and benefits than you ever dreamed. All you have to do is to design your own job, be productive, and be reliable. When you have done that, you may begin work. You can do anything you want as long as you are productive and reliable."

People have varying reactions ranging from cynicism ("life's not like that"), to confusion ("you know, I never thought like that"), to accurate precision ("you know, I've always wanted to do or be a. . . ."). Sometimes, they will grope for job titles, so the counselor might just say, "Well, how would you like to spend a single day or what would you like to do functionally to earn this attractive situation?" With respect to confusion and cynicism, the counselor simply can remind the client that this is a fantasy.

Having been a mental health and career counselor since 1972, Dr. Beck has found that as many as 80% of clients have a core set of functions or dream occupation that has perhaps never been discussed, been preempted because of unresolved problems, been seen as unattainable, or been shelved because of misinformation or discouragement from parents, teachers, friends, counselors, the media, or so-called objective career information. So the counselor then must ask once the core functions or dream aspirations are revealed, "What is getting in the way that you cannot realize these aspirations?" Be prepared for any number of real or perceived-as-real problems that the client may feel he or she never can surmount. Age, sex, religion, financial opportunity, poor grades, unsupportive environment, dissuasion by others, insecurity, not feeling worthy to aspire to such a profession or feeling that by ascribing to such a profession, would be seen by others as a poor career decision are among the reasons that are given frequently for not being able to achieve these aspirations.

Depending upon responses, the counselor now has much more useful information with which to help. If there is testing, the testing may be helpful in supporting the career fantasy. If results support other directions or compatible directions, the counselor can steer the client to additional information. The obligation of the counselor, however, is to help the client get where he or she really and truly desires to go. A secondary gain of this method is that the counselor can access more of the personal aspects of career decision, thus helping clients as individuals and not test results. This technique allows counselors to use actual personal as well as career counseling skills, which can be a winning combination. The challenge of the technique is to narrow the gap between fantasy and reality.

CHANGING CORE BELIEFS:
USE OF THE CORE BELIEF WORKSHEET

Therapist: Judith S. Beck, Ph.D.

Affiliation: Psychologist; Director of the Beck Institute for Cognitive Therapy and Research; Clinical Assistant Professor of Psychology in Psychiatry, University of Pennsylvania.

Major work:
>   Beck, J. S. (1995). *Cognitive therapy: Basics and beyond.* New York: Guilford.
>   Noted expert and lecturer in the field of cognitive therapy.

Population for whom the technique is appropriate: Adults.

Cautionary notes: None.

One of the most difficult challenges a therapist faces is helping clients change their most dysfunctional, deeply held, longstanding, rigid beliefs about themselves. These core beliefs often originated in childhood, were associated with either blatant or subtle but chronic trauma, and are part of the cognitive make-up of clients with personality disorders.

Core beliefs such as, "I am unlovable," "I am bad [or worthless]," "I am defective," "I am helpless," "I am vulnerable," "I am not good enough," or "I am incompetent" are difficult to modify because in many cases they are part of the client's identity. Personality disorder clients who hold a belief such as, "There is something fundamentally wrong with me," understand this belief to be "true" about themselves almost as strongly as they believe that they have a certain name, belong to a certain ethnic class, and are of a certain age. In fact, they believe the belief so strongly that they label it not as an idea but as a feeling: "I feel different" or "I feel like a failure." (Beck, 1995).

In order to modify core beliefs, the therapist first should help clients understand how it is possible to "feel" a core belief to be true, yet have it not be true or certainly not completely true. This task is made easier if clients have learned already that not all of their thinking is true and have had the experience of evaluating more modifiable cognitions, changing their thinking, and experiencing emotional relief from this rational appraisal. Next, the therapist offers a model of information processing that enables clients to recognize that they easily and automatically process negative information that is consistent with their core belief but fail to recognize or properly integrate positive data that is inconsistent with it (Beck, 1995).

The Core Belief Worksheet (Figure 3.1) helps clients monitor their progress in alternating the negative core beliefs and strengthening more functional, more realistic new beliefs. They rate the degree to which they believe these two sets of beliefs at the beginning of each session by completing the top of the worksheet.

Clients complete the rest of the worksheet throughout the week. When they recognize that their core belief has been activated—that is to say, when they start to feel bad, unlovable, helpless, inadequate, etc.—they record the situation, followed by an alternative explanation for the event. As illustrated in Figure 3.1, one client immediately felt as if he were a failure when he got a parking ticket, when he got only mildly positive feedback about an idea he presented at a staff meeting at work, and when he realized he had forgotten to buy dog food for his pet. When he "reframed" each experience by recording more realistic interpretations of what had happened, he felt significantly better.

On the left side of the worksheet, clients list experiences that contradict the negative core belief and support the new, more functional belief. For example, data that the client in Figure 3.1 is an okay person with strengths (and weaknesses) include his completing a difficult project at work, finishing his taxes, paying his bills, buying bonds with his savings, investigating a new automobile, and submitting his medical receipts to his insurance company. He recognized that a true failure could not have done any of these tasks successfully.

Consistent use of this worksheet week after week, in and between sessions, helps clients interpret their experiences in a more functional way and is an important part of the difficult process of chipping away at their very rigid negative beliefs. Over time, they solidify more realistic, functional views of themselves that positively influence behaviors and relationships.

References

Beck, J. S. (1995). *Cognitive therapy: Basics and beyond.* New York: Guilford.

Salkovskis, P. M. (Ed.). (1996). *Frontiers of cognitive therapy.* New York: Guilford.

Core Belief Worksheet

NAME:_____ DATE: _____

Old Core Belief: *I'm a failure.*

How much do you believe the old core belief right now? (0 to 100)__*80%*__
*What's the most you've believed it this week? (0 to 100)__*90%*__
*What's the least you've believed it this week? (0 to 100)___*50%*__

New Belief: *I'm okay. I have strengths and weaknesses.*

How much do you believe the new belief right now? (0 to 100)___*50%*__

Evidence That Contradicts Old Core Belief and Supports New Belief	**Evidence That Seems to Support Old Core Belief with Reframe**
1. Finished the loading project.	1. Got a parking ticket, BUT that happens to everyone from time to time, even to highly successful people.
2. Mailed in my taxes.	
3. Paid all outstanding bills.	
4. Looked into buying a Toyota.	
5. Bought savings bonds.	2. Got only slightly positive feedback on my idea at our staff meeting, BUT it was in the range of reasonable, and just because someone else came up with a better idea doesn't mean my idea was useless.
6. Mailed medical receipts.	
	3. Forgot to stop for dog food BUT did do three other errands. It's normal to forget things at times.

*Should situations related to an increase or decrease in the strength of the belief be topics for the agenda?

Figure 3.1. Example of Core Belief Worksheet used at the Beck Institute for Cognitive Therapy and Research. Copyright © 1996 by J. S. Beck, Ph.D.

FROM SUBTRACTION TO ADDITION

Therapists: Dorothy S. Becvar, Ph.D., & Raphael J. Becvar, Ph.D.

Affiliation: Dorothy Becvar—family therapist, LCSW, St. Louis Family Institute; Raphael Becvar—family therapist and psychologist, Northeast Louisiana University.

Major works:
> Becvar, D. S., & Becvar, R. J. (1994). *Hot chocolate for a cold winter's night: Essays for relationship development.* Denver, CO: Love Publishing.
> Becvar, D. S., & Becvar, R. J. (1996). *Family therapist: A systematic integration* (3rd ed.). Boston: Allyn & Bacon.

Population for whom the technique is appropriate: Any population.

Cautionary notes: None.

Counselors and therapists often see solving problems and reducing the incidence of mental illness as a process of subtraction. Accordingly, they join with the clients who wish to eliminate aspects or faults in themselves and/or their relationships. By contract, we find it much more useful to focus on the facilitation of health and wellness through a process of addition. Rather than trying to take away something old, we advocate putting in something new. Using a systemic story, we thus operate from the assumption that there is a limited amount of energy available to the client system, and the more energy devoted to the positive (addition), the less energy there is for the negative (subtraction).

Indeed, we have observed in our work with individuals, couples, and families that with an increase in the frequency of happy, helpful, and pleasurable experiences, there is a concomitant decrease in the incidence of the problem talk, problem behavior, and identification of problems. Thus, consistent with the other solution-focused practitioners, we ask questions, the answers to which orient clients toward addition and thereby engage in the co-creation of what we feel are more constructive therapeutic conversations.

The following are four examples of typical questions that we believe fall into the category of addition:

1. If your life (or relationship) were the way you would like it to be, what would be going on in very concrete, specific terms?
2. We have discussed at length those aspects of your life (or relationship) that you would like to change. What aspects of your life (or relationship) do you like and would you like to keep?
3. When things are (were) going well in your life (relationship), what are (were) you doing more of, less of, or differently?
4. We have talked at some length about the aspects of your life (or relationship) that you experience as problematic. I am curious about what is missing in your life (or relationship).

Increasingly, these questions also can be used by counselors and therapists to think about themselves and their work with clients. Indeed, we are as likely as our clients to get stuck from time to time. In such instances, it may be helpful to consider the questions we are asking, examine the assumptions we are making, and use a little addition with ourselves.

PSYCHODYNAMIC UNCOVERING TECHNIQUE (PUT)

Therapist: John D. Boyd, Ph.D., ABPH

Affiliation: Licensed Clinical Psychologist; Diplomate in Clinical Hypnosis, American Board of Psychological Hypnosis; private practice, Charlottesville, Virginia.

Major works:

> Bradley, L. & Boyd, J. D. (1989). *Counselor supervision: Approaches, preparation, practices.* Muncie, IN: Accelerated Development.
>
> Grieger, R. M., & Boyd, J. D. (1980). *Rational emotive therapy: A skills-based approach.* New York: Van Nostrand Reinhold.
>
> Author of numerous book chapters and journal articles on psychotherapy and clinical hypnosis.

Population for whom the technique is appropriate: A relaxation and suggestion technique for adolescent and adult clients.

Cautionary notes: Not recommended for clients who display major psychopathology.

Psychodynamic Uncovering Technique (PUT) is a relaxation and suggestive technique that encourages the easing of psychological defenses and the conscious experience and awareness of psychodynamics. Adolescent and adult clients who demonstrate at least an average amount of ego strength and emotional control are candidates for PUT; a high degree of psychopathology and/or manifest emotional disturbance is a contraindication. Clinicians employing the PUT within hypnotic procedure should be thoroughly trained in this modality (i.e., certification from the American Society of Clinical Hypnosis is recommended), and informed client consent is a prerequisite.

Theory and Rationale

According to the "psychodynamic principle," clients' symptoms are precipitated by and are expressions of subconscious psychodynamics (e.g., impulses, affect, perceptions, beliefs, behavioral predispositions). Psychological counseling and psychotherapy facilitate symptom reduction and personality growth by helping clients (a) bring unconscious material to conscious experience and awareness, (b) organize and express psychodynamic material, and (c) develop effective coping methods in the mediational and behavioral realm.

Procedures

Following the establishment of a therapeutic alliance, the psychodynamic principle is explained to the client as a natural and healthy phenomena, and the client is asked to participate in a relaxation exercise designed to facilitate psychodynamic uncovering and progress in therapy. Personalized relaxation instructions are offered, and when the client is in a deeply comfortable state, the clinician delivers a suggestive, psychoeducational narrative. In simple language and from the clinician's theoretical orientation, the narrative again explains the psychodynamic principle. The client is encouraged to allow, experience, uncritically accept, and explore within therapy those inner dynamics that he or she is psychologically ready to uncover for the purpose of resolving target symptoms and problems. The narrative is closed as the clinician voices his or her commitment to the therapeutic alliance and affirms the client's ability to use inner strengths and resources effectively for problem solving and constructive change within himself or herself.

A debriefing after the relaxation and narrative is accompanied by a suggested homework assignment: to maintain a daily diary of personally important incidents and experiences, particularly those in which symptoms arise. Diary material can be explored in subsequent therapy sessions, fostering skills of introspection and the experience, awareness, and expression of psychodynamics.

Outcome

The PUT promotes an empowering and ego strengthening form of psychological effort from clients, potentiating the counseling and psychotherapy process and decreasing symptomology (Boyd, 1994). Clients tend to lower resistances, bring meaningful experiential material to the clinician, and generally increase personal responsibility for their presenting problems and psychotherapy performance.

While the PUT emphasizes the psychodynamic principle and can be called a suggestive technique, it is forthright, psychoeducational, and compatible with most psychotherapy theories. Talented clinicians can adapt the PUT to fit clients' personality styles, symptoms, and problem contexts.

Reference

Boyd, J. D. (1994). Potentiating group psychotherapy for bulimia with ancillary rational-emotive hypnotherapy. *Journal of Rational Emotive and Cognitive-Behavior Therapy, 12*(4), 229-236.

HUMILITY, AUGMENTED BY THE
DEEP BREATH TECHNIQUE

Therapist: Peter R. Breggin, M.D.

Affiliation: Psychiatrist, National Director, Center for the Study of Psychiatry and Psychology, Bethesda, Maryland; Faculty Associate, The John Hopkins University Department of Counseling and Human Services, Baltimore, Maryland.

Major works:
> Breggin, P. R. (1991). *Why therapy, empathy, and love must replace the drugs, electroshock, and biochemical theories of the "new psychiatry."* New York: St. Martin's Press.
> Breggin, P. R. (1994). *Talking back to Prozac: What doctors aren't telling you about today's most controversial drugs.* New York: St. Martin's Press.
> Breggin, P. R. (1997). *The heart of being helpful: Empathy and the creation of healing aura.* New York: Springer.
> Author of many other books.

Population for whom the technique is appropriate: Any population.

Cautionary notes: None.

Although I am probably not the first psychiatrist or psychotherapist to employ humility as a technique, I have been unable to find any references to it in the professional literature. Perhaps mental health professionals are so naturally humble that they seldom need to think about it. Humility can be augmented by what I call "the deep breath technique."

The *American Heritage Dictionary* (1992) defines humility as the quality or condition of being humble. Humble, itself, is defined as "marked by meekness or modesty in behavior, attitude, or spirit; not arrogant or prideful." Other meanings of humble include "low" and "submissive." Perhaps these latter connotations have discouraged some psychiatrists and therapists from embracing it.

While humility can become an active technique, often it seems to erupt spontaneously during therapy. When one of our clients has a major insight without our help, for example, we may feel humbled. After all, why didn't we think of it first?

Given that humility often happens to us, more or less out of our control, can we make it into an active therapeutic intervention? Yes, we can. In fact, if we cannot consciously turn to humility as a technique, we are likely to do more harm than good in our work.

It is especially important to become humble when we feel frustrated with our patients and want to use a special technique on them. John, for example, may not seem to be benefitting from regular "talk therapy." And so we start searching through our arsenal of special techniques—everything from hypnosis and behavioral modification to facial expressions that suggest "I'm doing the best I can—so what's the matter with you?" As a humbling alternative, we might ask John, "I'm not sure I'm being as useful to you as I can be. Do *you* think there's something I can do to be more helpful to you?"

Whenever we feel especially judgmental toward one of our clients, humility once again becomes a useful technique. For example, we may be tempted to say something that suggests, however indirectly, "I would never have done something so stupid, so harmful, as you did." The *deep breath technique* can prove especially useful at such a time in augmenting humility. In this technique, we take a deep breath, keep our mouth shut, and repeat to ourselves, "I might have done something even more stupid and harmful."

Humility is often useful when diagnosing our clients. Subtle distinctions between schizophrenia, schizophreniform disorder, schizoaffective disorder, schizotypal personality disorder, and schizoid personality disorder can indeed be intriguing. The mental exercise of making such a "differential diagnosis" does seem to help many psychiatrists and psychotherapists feel better about themselves. But humility would tempt us to ask, "Will a diagnosis encourage John and Jill to feel better about themselves? Will it help us appreciate our common humanity with John and Jill?" If we ask such questions, we may find, in all humility, that it is best to give up making diagnoses. That probably will encourage us to learn more about the actual lives of our patients, their unique stories that defy artificial categories and diagnoses.

When John or Jill "doesn't respond to psychotherapy," humility is a preferred technique to recommending medication. We should consider the possibility, however remote, that the fault in the therapy, if any, lies in ourselves rather than in our clients. Perhaps it is time for self-insight, if not self-medication, and time for a consultation with one of our colleagues about how to be more helpful to John or to Jill.

In therapy, it can seem difficult to understand how our clients have become so overwhelmed with feelings of fear and helplessness. John and Jill may at times seem inexcusably weak to us. At these moments, we need to work harder to understand what John and Jill have endured in their lives. Almost surely, we've been lucky by comparison. After using the deep breath technique to augment our humility—that is, after taking a deep breath and keeping our mouth shut—we can remind ourselves, "There but for the grace of God go I."

Too many times as therapists we act as if our patients should be grateful for our help. Humility teaches us that we are the ones who should be grateful for the opportunity to know and to help such interesting and wonderful human beings while even getting paid for it. The grateful therapist is probably a more effective therapist.

Humility does have its limitations. Many of our patients, for example, initially feel so frightened and overwhelmed that they seem to beg us to do something to manipulate and to control them. These patients may feel comfortable with our usual psychiatric and psychotherapeutic techniques.

As any powerful technique, humility can be overused. If we become too humble, we may find ourselves empowering our patients rather than ourselves, encouraging their sense of worth and their independent capacity to make decisions. They then may decide for themselves that they do not like our favorite techniques, including my own attempts at humility. They may seek more effective help elsewhere. They even may conclude that they do not need any further mental health interventions in their lives.

Humility, like other effective approaches in therapy, is something that takes place inside ourselves as therapists rather than inside our patients or clients. Yet it can have a powerful, healing influence on the people we are helping. As I did my best to describe in *The Heart of Being Helpful: Empathy and the Creation of Healing Presence* (1997), it is often more healing to do something to ourselves than to our clients.

The more empathy we feel toward others, the more humble we are likely to feel about ourselves. John and Jill, for example, probably have a lot more to them than we ever anticipated. They probably have overcome stresses and trauma that would have flattened us. But they need encouragement. Merely by being humble in their presence, we are likely to inspire them.

References

American Heritage Dictionary. (1992). New York: Houghton-Mifflin.

Breggin, P. R. (1997). *The heart of being helpful: Empathy and the creation of healing aura.* New York: Springer.

HYPNOTICALLY ENHANCED INTERACTIVE COGNITIVE REHEARSAL

Therapist: W. Gary Cannon, Ph.D.

Affiliation: Director, Anxiety & Stress Disorder Program, Professor of Psychology, California School of Professional Psychology-Fresno; private practice.

Major works:

Bent, R. J., & Cannon, W. G. (1987). Key functional skills of a professional psychologist. In R. Bourg, R. Bent, J. Callan, N. Jones, J. McHolland, & G. Stricker (Eds.), *Standard and evaluation in the education and training of professional psychologists: Knowledge, attitudes, and skills* (pp. 87-97). National Council of Schools of Professional Psychology. Norman, OK: Transcript Press.

Cannon, W. G., & McHolland, J. D. (1991). Core curricular change: Barriers and strategies for achieving meaningful change. In R. L. Peterson, J. D. McHolland, R. J. Bent, E. Davis-Russell, G. E. Edwall, K. Polite, D. L. Singer, & G. Stricker (Eds.), *The core curriculum in professional psychology* (pp. 69-74). Washington, DC: American Psychological Association.

Templer, D. I., Hartlage, L. C., & Cannon, W. G. (1992). *Preventable brain damage: Brain vulnerability and brain health.* New York: Springer.

Author of 10 other book chapters and articles.

Population for whom the technique is appropriate: This technique is ideal for clients with fears, phobic reactions, anxiety disorders, and obsessive-compulsive disorders.

Cautionary notes: Training in hypnosis and systematic desensitization is recommended.

Procedure

Combining hypnosis, visual imagery, exposure therapy, coping skills development, and cognitive rehearsal in an interactive format, this approach has produced surprisingly consistent positive results across a wide range of patients and problems. It is particularly well-suited to the treatment of phobic avoidance, such as assisting patients to overcome fears of flying. It is effective in helping patients prepare for courtroom testimony and other high pressure forms of public speaking such as conducting seminars and presentations. In addition, it is very useful for helping patients prepare for in vivo exposure sessions with agoraphobia, social phobia, and obsessive-compulsive disorder.

The method is simple and straightforward. Prior to the hypnotic induction, the therapist should establish a "safe place image." The safe place image is a scene or situation that for the patient is tranquil, peaceful, and relaxing. Most people choose a beach, ocean, or mountain scene. The mountain scenes usually also involve water such as a lake, a waterfall, or a stream. Some individuals select their bedroom or a special room in their home where they can relax, read, meditate, or just kick back. The therapist should elicit details of the image. Next the therapist inquires regarding the feared scene or situation to be overcome, again collecting enough details to allow a vivid recreation by the therapist.

Following a standard hypnotic induction utilizing progressive muscular relaxation, allow the patient to experience the safe place image, describing it in detail. While the patient is visualizing the image, ask pertinent questions regarding the scene to flesh it out more fully. After the patient is sufficiently relaxed, shift to the anxiety provoking scene or situation, also describing it in some detail. Invite the patient to visualize himself or herself as a part of the picture, as though he or she were observing from a distance ("a fly on the wall") or as though he or she were seeing the scene on a movie screen. For particularly traumatic scenes, the patient is encouraged to feel somewhat insulated from the scene, not to allow himself or herself to be overwhelmed by it, but just to experience a level of emotion that he or she can handle. The patient should be encouraged now to observe himself or herself as being confident and competent and as coping with the feared situation as it is described by the therapist. The scenario can be played and replayed a number of times. As the therapist details the imagery, inquiries are made to determine what the patient is seeing and experiencing. During the processing of this imaginal exposure, the therapist next includes some complication or unexpected problem such as turbulence (if dealing with fear of flying) or a hostile member of the audience (if preparing for a presentation). These problems may derail the patient momentarily, but either on his or her own or with the aide of the therapist, the patient will recover, regain composure, and continue.

The recovery is achieved by invoking coping skills such as the safe place imagery or by taking a few deep breaths if deep breathing has been taught as a coping skill. The therapist asks the patient to describe in detail what is happening, and in cases where there is trouble recovering from the more anxiety producing aspects of the exposure, the therapist uses the power of hypnotic suggestion and hypnotic deepening techniques until the patient can return to the scene and visualize himself or herself coping adequately with the problem.

Next the therapist may invite the patient to visualize the scene as though he or she were actually there experiencing it firsthand. Again, the scene can be replayed as necessary until the patient is successful. The interactive nature of this procedure allows the therapist to be creative in helping the patient find solutions and overcome obstacles. My experience is that patients who cannot visualize themselves successfully coping with the feared scene will not cope with the *in vivo* situation either. Thus, it is imperative to work with the imagery until the patient succeeds. Verbal feedback from the patient gives the therapist important clues regarding the most appropriate coping strategy. Obviously, the procedure works best with patients who are able to visualize and who are at least moderately susceptible to hypnosis. These criteria are met by well over 70% of the population. Also, the method seems to be particularly effective with patients who have a deadline that toward which they are working. For this reason, if no natural deadline exists, it often is useful to schedule one and then stick to it. For example, ask the patient to purchase a non-refundable airline ticket one month or so in advance, and then use several sessions or more as needed to prepare for the flight.

Rationale for the Procedure

It is well-established that hypnosis can enhance the effectiveness of many cognitive and behavioral procedures (Rhue, Lynn, & Kirsch, 1993). Moreover, its addition here allows a deeper relaxation response, more vivid visual imagery, and greater access to affective responses.

Allen Bergin published an article (Bergin, 1969) demonstrating an enhanced effect with systematic desensitization by encouraging patients to talk about the scenes in the desensitization hierarchy. This discussion or interaction seemed to serve as a desensitization process in and of itself. The interactive nature of the present procedure capitalizes on that effect and is strengthened further when combined with hypnosis. The idea of viewing oneself as "on a screen" was inspired by the work of Bandura and Mahoney utilizing modeling procedures to treat phobias. It is well-known that when models are used to treat phobias, greater similarity between the model and the patient leads to greater treatment efficacy (Mahoney, 1974). Using this idea, Mahoney videotaped patients attempting difficult and frightening tasks, edited the tapes leaving the most competent and successful looking segments, played them back for the patients, and thus used the patient as his or her own model. The present technique builds on the same principle but does it through visualization of self as model in a coping context.

References

Bergin, A. E. (1969). A technique for improving desensitization via warmth, empathy and emotional reexperiencing of hierarchy events. In R. Rubin & C. M. Franks (Eds.), *Advances in behavior therapy* (pp. 117–130). New York: Academic Press.

Mahoney, M. J. (1974). *Cognitive and behavior modification.* Cambridge, MS: Ballinger.

Rhue, J. W., Lynn, S. J., & Kirsch, I. (Eds.). (1993). *Handbook of clinical hypnosis.* Washington, DC: American Psychological Association.

Editor's Note: I was deeply saddened by the fact that Dr. Cannon died suddenly on January 11, 1997, after undergoing surgery before the publication of this text. My sympathy goes out to his family, friends, and colleagues. He was excited about the fact that his technique was chosen for the book, and several months prior to his death, we discussed the fact that he and I were the only contributors who submitted a hypnotic strategy.

LIFELINE

Therapist: Victoria D. Coleman, Ed.D.

Affiliation: Licensed Psychologist (Michigan); Licensed Marriage and Family Therapist (Indiana); Licensed Clinical Social Worker (Indiana); Registered Professional Career Counselor (California); National Certified Counselor; National Certified Career Counselor; National Certified Gerontological Counselor; Clinical Member, American Association for Marriage and Family Therapy; Purdue University; private practice.

Major works:
> Coleman, V. D., & Farris-Dufrene, P. H. (1996). *Art therapy and psychotherapy: Blending two therapeutic approaches.* Muncie IN: Accelerated Development.
> Author of a book chapter and 40 articles in counseling and career development journals.

Population for whom the technique is appropriate: Children, adolescents, and adults in individual, family, and group sessions. Also applicable for education, business, industry, government, community agencies, and organizations. For example, one might do a Lifeline of an organization or business.

Cautionary notes: The Lifeline should be utilized with caution in that sometimes an individual might divulge extremely personal situations that would require intensive follow-up with a mental health professional. It is important to discuss these incidents in order to protect the integrity of the exercise and the well-being of the individual involved in writing his or her Lifeline.

The purpose of the therapeutic technique called the Lifeline is to allow individuals (organizations, businesses, etc.) to explore their past and present, and make projections for the future. It provides information to assist individuals in identifying the themes, trends, and patterns in their lives.

The following instructions are given to the individual, group, class, family, etc., in order to complete the Lifeline. These instructions should be given in writing and orally.

Lifeline

The purpose of the Lifeline is to assist individuals in examining their past and present, and to make some projections for the future. During this process, one will be able to discern themes, patterns, and trends in the Lifeline, which should provide additional information about one's behavior. This activity probably will take an extended period of time to complete (i.e., a few hours, days); therefore, prior to beginning to write the Lifeline, one should give it serious thought.

1. Draw a Lifeline of yourself. The Lifeline should be how you perceive yourself. Remember that a line can take a variety of shapes and forms (i.e., it does not have to be straight).
2. Begin somewhere in the past, and project to some point in the future. Start with your earliest memory, and project to at least one year from today.
3. Note the significant events that have shaped your life. These events do not have to be earth-shattering but still can represent milestones (e.g., learning to ride a two-wheel bicycle, going on a first date, etc.).
4. For clarification, use the following symbols to further illustrate your Lifeline:
   ! = a risk or chance that you took
   X = an obstacle—something (or someone) that prevented you from getting or doing what you wanted
   O = a decision made for you by somebody else
   + = a positive, satisfying, or appropriate decision
   – = a negative, unsatisfying, or inappropriate decision
   ? = a decision that you anticipate making in the future (i.e., up to two years from now)

You may use any or all of the symbols as often as you like. A particular event could have all six (6) symbols for further clarification. Also, feel free to create symbols that represent your particular experiences.

After the individual indicates that the Lifeline is completed, the counselor should allow the individual to discuss the Lifeline in detail. The counselor should ask for feedback and clarification of various events and statements made on the Lifeline.

The Lifeline is an excellent way to begin the counseling process. It can be a very significant tool when clients are reticent, are unable to articulate their thoughts and feelings, or have apprehensions about the counseling process. The Lifeline is also appropriate at any stage of the counseling process and should be used as a frame of reference for establishing counseling goals and objectives.

Note: I am not certain of the origin of this activity; therefore, I do not claim ownership with respect to the development of the Lifeline. I have, however, used it for approximately 15 years with a variety of populations in education, business, industry, government, community agencies, and professional associations. All populations have responded quite favorably to the Lifeline.

TURNING THE TABLES ON THE CLIENT: MAKING THE CLIENT THE COUNSELOR

Therapist: Raymond J. Corsini, Ph.D.

Affiliation: Retired private practice clinical and industrial psychologist.

Major works:

Corsini, R. J., & Wedding, D. (1994). *Current psychotherapies.* Itaska, IL: F. E. Peacock.

Corsini, R. J., & Wedding, D. (1987). *Encyclopedia of psychology.* Canada: John Wiley and Sons.

Painter, G., & Corsini, R. J. (1990). *Effective discipline in the home and school.* Muncie, IN: Accelerated Development.

Author and editor of over 25 books and numerous professional articles.

Cautionary notes: All techniques, of course, have to be used with wisdom and judgment. This particular technique calls for a lot of savvy about human nature in general and the specific person or persons and the situation.

In some 50 years of experience as a counselor and a psychotherapist, what has annoyed me more than anything else is when a client rejects my diagnosis or my suggestion, or my counseling, saying that it does not work, it will not work, they do not like it, etc. In dealing with such people, I have used a number of strategies, and I shall summarize some quickly and then discuss one at length.

I'll Betcha

One of these techniques is called "I'll Betcha." It goes as follows: Say that I suggest that a client do a particular thing to achieve a particular end and the client says it will not work. I will persist and finally will say, "I'll betcha it will." Then I outline the bet—always for exactly $2.00. If the client accepts my bet, the conditions are the following: He or she is to do exactly what I say. If it does not work, he or she wins the bet; if it does work, I win the bet. I have made about 50 such bets over the years and have not lost one. The interesting part is that my opponent decides whether it worked or not.

Give Up

Another powerful technique is to give up. The client opposes me on something, and if I am planning to use this technique, I begin to manipulate the client by doing some low-level arguing or attempting to explain the procedure to a greater extent, but never trying to overwhelm the person, letting him or her think that he or she is convincing me. Finally, I say, "I think you may be right. But I cannot accept your reasoning, and you cannot accept mine. For that reason, I suggest you get yourself a better counselor, someone who will agree with you. You do not have to pay for this session."

In practically every case, the client is thrown off the track, apologizes, begs me to keep him or her as a client, and I shake my head and say, "I have given you my best advice." Now we are in a new conflict with the client wanting me to stay and me saying I want to go, and I change the discussion to the issue of difference until the client agrees to try it.

Nuts and Bolts of the Turning the Tables Technique

Essentially, this technique can be used in two situations: One, when you, the counselor or therapist, are not sure what to do. You may feel like taking the Carl Rogers approach and stall the situation, hoping that somehow something will emerge from the counselee that will be of value. The second situation in which this technique can be used is when the counselee is convinced that what you are advising will not work, and you have respect for the counselee's intelligence and judgment.

So, you come to a situation that is kind of a dead end. At this point, you stand up (and if you are behind a desk, you come in front of it) and say, "Would you mind standing up?" and you wait until your puzzled counselee stands up also.

You then move around the person so that you now will be 180 degrees from where you were standing (now facing your chair). The counselee turns also (if necessary, nudge or touch the person) until you are facing each other again but now he or she has his or her back to your original chair. Now you say: "I want you to take my chair and sit down." You wait until the person does just that. Should the person ask why, you refuse to answer the first request. Simply look at the client and smile. If there is a second request to know why, say, "I'll tell you as soon as you sit down." And you wait. In some cases, you may have to wait several minutes. Finally, in most cases, the puzzled client will sit down. Then you say: "I am going out of the room for about 10 seconds. When I return, you will be me and I will be you. We will meet for the first time, and I will tell you my problem and you be the counselor."

Without waiting for an answer or answering any questions, you leave the room, close the door, come back in, and you are now the *client.* You enter, give your name (the client's name), and wait standing up until finally your client who is now *your counselor* asks you to sit down. You now act exactly as you would have were you that person, thereby forcing the counselee to act as a counselor. Eventually you come to the central problem, asking the "counselor" for suggestions, advice, etc.

The "counselor" may attempt to avoid being put in this spot and in some cases will get up from the chair, etc., but once *you* have started to play the role of the *counselee,* you are to maintain that role until you go out the door and come back as the *counselor.*

Now, what happens in some cases is that the two of you begin to have a dialogue and should your "counselor" suggest what you originally had suggested you now will oppose the ideas with, if possible, the very same terms that the original counselee used.

This continues until you believe the charade is over, go out of the door, come back in, and, best using only gestures not words, indicate that the counselee return to his or her original chair. Upon reseating yourself, ask, "What do you think?" or some other related open-ended question.

This procedure, when it works, works quite well. The former "counselor" (i.e., the client) often will see things from a new perspective—you role-playing him or her—and may realize that the advice, suggestions, etc. you originally had given do make sense. It can establish a new and better level of relationship of greater equality and increase the bond between you and your counselee.

On the other hand, if not handled with finesse and confidence, and if the person you try this with gets upset, you may lose the counselee. I never have experienced this, but then I have used this procedure only when I am certain it will work. Let me give one case history as an example.

Example of The Turning the Tables Technique Working

A woman had come to me because her son was doing poorly in school. I examined school records, psychologists' reports, and interviewed the boy briefly. It was obvious that he was not a bright child. At one point, I suggested to the mother that she give up her goal to have her son go to college and become a professional and that she consider having her son engage in his father's profession—he laid tile and carpets. She replied: "Better he should die!"

This mother's sole aim was to get me to teach her how to motivate her son, and my recital of his wretched school history, psychological test results, and my impression of him had no effect on her. She was an intelligent woman, a strong and determined person, and so I decided to try this reversal method. I got up, so did she, we turned around, she took my seat, and I went out, came back, and stood up. The dialogue (as best as I can remember) went as follows:

> **Client acting as the counselor:** *Please take a seat.* (I sat down and remained silent.) *Why are you here?*
> **Corsini acting as the client:** *My son is not doing well in school. He is getting poor grades.*
> **Client acting as the counselor:** *What is the explanation?*
> **Corsini acting as the client:** *I don't know. I don't think he studies enough.*
> **Client acting as the counselor:** *What do you do?*
> **Corsini acting as the client:** *Everything I can think of. I tell him how important education is to a young man. I tell him how proud I am when he does well. I tell him how smart he is. I do everything I can.*
> **Client acting as the counselor:** *What does he do?*
> **Corsini acting as the client:** *He cries and says he does the best he can. But I tell him I love him and want him to do better.*

At this point my "counselor" broke down into tears. I waited in silence, and when she recovered, I went out of the room, came back, pointed her to her original chair, and sat down. The session continued somewhat as follows:

> **Client:** *I said he should die rather than do what my husband does?*

I nodded. Then the conversation turned to the fact that she looked down on her husband because he had never gone past high school, and she did not want her son to be like his father. She realized that she was mistreating her son by requesting more of him than it was possible for him to do. We continued our counseling, but the important thing was that via this shifting of roles she came to realize how unfair she had been relative to both her husband and her son.

Naturally, the same results might have occurred using other techniques, but sometimes this reversal works apparent miracles.

THE USE OF SYMBOLS AND RITUALS
IN PSYCHOTHERAPY

Therapist: Richard H. Cox, Ph.D., ABPP

Affiliation: Clinical Psychologist, President, Forest Institute of Professional Psychology, Springfield, Missouri.

Major works:

Cox, R. (Ed.). (1973). *Religious systems and psychotherapy.* Springfield, IL: Charles C. Thomas.

Cox, R. H., & Esau, T. G. (1974). *Regressive therapy: Therapeutic regression of schizophrenic children and young adults.* New York: Brunner-Mazel.

Author of numerous chapters in books and articles in professional journals.

Population for whom the technique is appropriate: Any population.

Cautionary notes: None.

Psychotherapy is inevitably entangled with the relationship of the present to the past and the future. It is most often the mistakes and problems of the past that bring a patient to therapy. Building the bridge from the past to the present always has presented a challenge. Whether it is done by psychoanalysis or by behavioral means, the patient must find ways to "be done with the past" and "get on with the future." The author has found that by utilizing symbols and rituals, the process can be shortened and deepened at the same time. A single symbol has meaning in and of itself, and a combination of symbols makes a ritual. Both call for the utilization of basic relationships to persons, places, and life happenings. Symbols and rituals may be religious or not, but they are always "spiritual." The psychotherapeutic functions of symbol and ritual are as follows:

1. They provide a process by which one may bridge years, relationships, and multiple events in one's life.
2. They allow for a process by which one may gain insight and understanding of both present and past relationships without multiple sessions of probing.
3. They promote a process by which one may reconstruct and repair breaches in past and present relationships.

4. They provide meaning to myth, allowing one to return to a healthy person within one's self and one's family.
5. They provide a framework within which one can bring emotional healing regardless of the wishes and/or participation of others.

Symbols and rituals utilize already accepted beliefs to deal with the unaccepted, allow one to identify with a value base without putting it into words, discourage argumentation since symbols have an absolute meaning to the individual and usually to society, and do not permit analysis. A symbol and/or a ritual is deeply emotional and secondarily intellectual; therefore, a quick and often easy route is found into the ability to abreact, cathart, and reconstruct with a kind of insight that transcends both time and space.

It is important to take the following steps to assure the effective use of symbols and rituals:

1. Name the problem. Traditional psychotherapy has been slow to "name" things and would rather use "diagnosis," which has little if any meaning to the patient. The "demon" needs to be named.
2. Search for a symbol that bridges the problem area. Take, for instance, a patient who had an unfulfilling relationship with his father and was not rewarded as a child when he sang a solo in church that had to do with a dove. This patient found a tie-tack of a dove that became the symbol of re-engagement.
3. The patient needs to be encouraged and led into participation in new and sometimes unfamiliar processes first starting with clearly understood symbols such as a wedding band, a church spire, or a traffic stop sign. When the meaning of this kind of symbol is established, the patient then may be led to understand the importance of symbol to life and how symbols contribute and sometimes control behavior.
4. The patient then is assisted in identifying the specific symbol(s) and ritual that will bridge the "demonic" area. Sometimes the demon is not accepting the death of a parent, in which case a trip to the cemetery may be essential in order to find an object that pulls the patient and the deceased parent into a symbolic unity.
5. No object is too extreme to be acceptable as a symbol. The therapist does not need to understand the relationship, so long as the patient does. The therapist must lead the exploration and rejoice with the patient when the symbol is found.
6. The symbol and ritual must be memorialized in some fashion. This may take the form of a letter that later is destroyed, a trip to a burial site, a re-solemnization of wedding vows, the wearing of a ring or piece

of jewelry, the mounting of a picture in a conspicuous place, or a myriad of other possibilities.

Symbol related psychotherapy offers particular advantage in this day of managed care and emphasis upon short-term approaches. Because symbols and rituals tend to become highly individualized, they offer bridges and bonds that although are established quickly are often permanent. The use of symbols brings about a reification (i.e., a transformation of abstract feelings into the concrete) and a methods by which to return to painful experiences with the ability to move on to the future with a positively charged emotionality. Every patient is seeking a way to "start over again." The use of symbols and rituals allows such an opportunity.

THE SAEB SYSTEM
(SYMPTOMS, AUTOMATIC THOUGHTS, EMOTIONS, AND BEHAVIOR) IN THE TREATMENT AND CONCEPTUALIZATION OF PANIC ATTACKS

Therapist: Frank M. Dattilio, Ph.D., ABPP

Affiliation: Clinical psychologist; Department of Psychiatry, University of Pennsylvania School of Medicine and The Center for Integrative Psychotherapy.

Major works:
> Dattilio, F. M., & Freeman, A. (Eds.). (1994). *Cognitive-behavioral strategies in crisis intervention.* New York: Guilford.
>
> Freeman, A., & Dattilio, F. M. (Eds.). (1992). *Comprehensive casebook of cognitive therapy.* New York: Plenum.
>
> Reinecke, A., Dattilio, F. M., & Freeman, A. (Eds.). (1995). *Cognitive therapy with children and adolescents: A casebook for clinical practices.* New York, Guilford.
>
> Author of two other books and over 70 professional articles and book chapters.

Population for whom the technique is appropriate: Children (over the age of 12), adolescents,and adults.

Cautionary notes: None.

Panic attacks and panic disorder can sometimes prove to be a treatment challenge for the practicing clinician. This is particularly true with patients who experience atypical symptoms or difficulty in explaining the onset and course of their attacks. The following pages introduce a useful exploratory and therapeutic technique for treating the patient with panic attack or panic disorder. The reader is referred to the *Diagnostic and Statistical Manual for Mental Disorders, Revised* (DSM-III-R) for a description of the criteria for a diagnosis of panic attacks. The DSM-IV, published in May, 1994, includes an additional condition which emphasizes that the attacks must escalate to a specified level of severity within a period of 10 minutes. In addition, the specification of a certain number of panic attacks has been eliminated, and the feature of being unexpected or "out of the blue" has been emphasized.

There are a number of theories regarding the etiology of panic attacks. One is the cognitive theory proposed by Clark (1986). The cognitive theory of panic states that panic attacks result from catastrophic misinterpretation of certain bodily sensations that serve as signs of an imminent physical or mental disaster such as experiencing a heart attack or losing control of one's faculties (Beck, Emery, & Greenberg, 1985; Clark, 1986). Current cognitive-behavioral literature on anxiety stresses the importance of identifying symptoms of panic, specific interoceptive cues, and cognitive distortions (Alford, Beck, Freeman, & Wright, 1990; Dattilio, 1986, 1992a; 1992b; 1994a; Ehlers, 1993; Ottaviani & Beck, 1987; Solkol, Beck, Greenberg, Wright, & Berchick, 1989).

Barlow's (1988) biopsychosocial approach places emphasis on the initial panic attack as a misfiring of the fear system under stressful life circumstances in physiologically and psychologically vulnerable individuals. Physiological vulnerability is conceptualized as a set of danger-laden beliefs about bodily sensations and the world in general (Craske & Barlow, 1993). Barlow (1988) and Wolpe and Rowan (1988) suggest that the traumatic nature of the first panic attack and the consequent learning that takes place play a major role in the reoccurrence of subsequent attacks.

The cognitive-behavioral perspective on panic has been combined therapeutically with behavioral strategies, particularly when symptoms of phobic avoid-ance develop (Barlow, 1988). The essential goal of cognitive-behavior therapy (CBT) is to reduce and eventually extinguish the association of heightened panic attacks and the somatic, cognitive, affective, and behavioral components that con-tribute to the escalating panic spiral.

Current CBT treatment regimens include the use of psychoeducational techniques for helping patients understand the nature and properties of panic and anxiety (Dattilio & Kendall, 1994). These regimens also stress the use of cognitive restructuring for the misinterpretation of interoceptive cues plus methods of symptom induction, breathing retraining, de-escalation (the reduction of the intensity of symptoms), and the use of anxiolytic medication in a combined treatment package (Clark, 1986; Dattilio & Berchick, 1992; Dattilio & Kendall, in press; Sanderson & Wetzler, 1993; Solkol et al., 1989). The effectiveness of such techniques has been demonstrated not only through extensive case study material (Alford et al., 1990; Dattilio, 1986; Dattilio, in press; Dattilio & Berchick, 1992; Greenberg, 1989), but through empirical investigations and well-controlled outcome studies as well (Beck, Solkol, Clark, Berchick, & Wright, 1992; Klosko, Barlow, Tassinari, & Cerny, 1990; Michelson, Marchione, Greenwald, Glanz, Testa, & Marchione, 1990; Solkol et al., 1989).

Although many of the symptoms of panic are similar for those who experience attacks, the cognitions and affect may fluctuate, producing some variations in the overall behavioral display of the attack. These symptoms often occur so spontaneously and in such rapid succession that panic sufferers are unable to identify the sequence of escalation. In addition, they may avoid thinking about it for fear of eliciting a subsequent attack. For successful cognitive-behavioral intervention, it is helpful for the clinician and the patient to accurately comprehend and conceptualize the sequence of inner events that occur during an episode from the onset of anxiety to the full-blown panic attack. Furthermore, it is important, from a treatment standpoint, to identify what symptoms the patient interprets as being dangerous, because panic appears at times to result in more catastrophic thought content than with many of the other subtypes of anxiety disorders (Dattilio, 1986). This assignment of danger is an important target in the treatment component.

The technique proposed here, SAEB, is intended to facilitate the CBT therapeutic process. It provides a practical system for conceptualizing panic attacks that delineates the victim's personal sequence of events and then tracks the course of their panic escalation. This appears to be something that has been lacking in previous treatment approaches.

SAEB System

The system of conceptualization detailed in this paper is called the "SAEB System" (for symptoms, automatic thoughts, emotion, and behavior). The acronym describes the elements reported by many panic victims as giving rise to their alarm.

The SAEB system was developed as a result of numerous clinical cases in which panic sufferers demonstrated frustration of their attempts to convey to others, including the treating clinician, the exact sequence of events during an attack. The difficulty generally arises from the fact that the events occur so rapidly and spontaneously that panic sufferers are unable to pinpoint their symptoms or their thoughts and emotions. Therefore, a structured system may be needed to aid practitioners and patients in tracking the sequence of the panic episodes (Craske & Barlow, 1993, p. 6).

The SAEB system is applied by having patients identify the initial symptom or symptoms that precipitate the panic episode (Dattilio, 1994b). These symptoms are elicited by utilizing such inventories as the Beck Anxiety Inventory (BAI) (Beck, 1987), the Body Sensations Questionnaire (BSQ) (Chambless, Caputo, Bright, & Gallagher, 1984), or other empirically derived panic measures, supplemented by Socratic questioning during the interview phase. If the individual has experienced more than one attack, uncovering the SAEB sequence can help expose the repetitive character of the attacks. If the recollection of symptoms presents a problem, either because the patient is blocking or simply has poor recall, then the use of panic induction exercises may be helpful as defined by Clark (1986) and portrayed in additional case studies in the literature (Alford et al., 1990; Dattilio & Berchick, 1992; Dattilio & Kendall, 1994). Panic induction often is used as part of the assessment phase in cases where the individual experiences difficulty in recalling the exact sequences of symptoms. The use of breathing retraining and progressive relaxation exercises should be taught and then practiced by the patient in order to de-escalate bodily symptoms during the panic induction technique and also later on during the course of any spontaneous panic in or outside of the therapy session.

Once the systems and their sequence (e.g., heart palpitations, shortness of breath, lightheadedness, etc.) have been established, the therapist applies the SAEB system by aligning these symptoms with specific automatic thoughts and accompanying emotions and behaviors. These can be obtained firsthand by using the panic induction exercise or through the patient's own reports in a *Weekly Panic Log* (Center for Cognitive Therapy, Philadelphia).

The assembled sequence of panic attack elements—symptoms, automatic thoughts, emotion, and behavior—can then be represented in a diagram as a teaching tool to help show the patient how automatic thoughts and their accompanying emotions work to escalate the attack.

Using information from the following case vignette of "Rosemary," the three illustrations show how patient and clinician collaboratively map out the stages of the attack. Figure 3.2 demonstrates how an "abrupt increase in heart rate" was the initial symptom experienced at the onset of each attack for Rosemary. This was followed by "an increase and difficulty in breathing" and subsequently by lightheadedness and sweating in Figure 3.3 and so on in Figure 3.4. Once the symptoms were aligned, the automatic thoughts accompanying each system were listed in a corresponding vertical column. Finally, the associated emotion and behavior were listed in a third vertical column. Vectors were then drawn in order to demonstrate to Rosemary in a collaborative fashion how the catastrophic thought content may occur in reaction to the autonomic symptoms and how these thoughts contribute to the subsequent behavior and to the subsequent escalation of the symptoms (Dattilio, 1992a). This technique is demonstrated in detail in a previous case study (Dattilio & Berchick, 1992) and is also outlined in detail below where a panic induction exercise is used to retrieve symptoms which are then charted through the SAEB system.

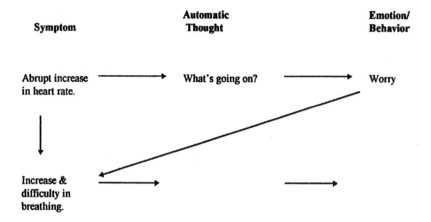

Figure 3.2.   Phase 1 of panic sequence.

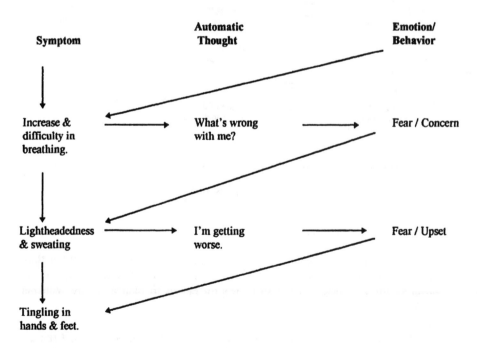

Figure 3.3.   Phase 2 of panic sequence.

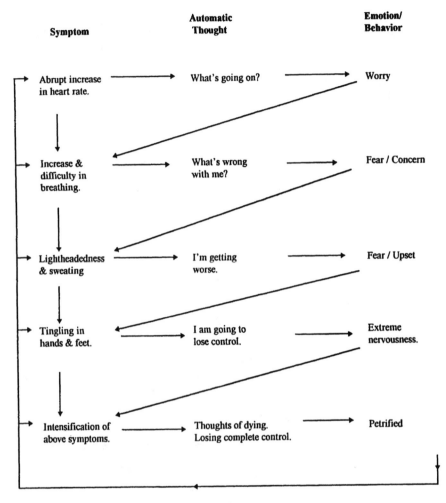

Figure 3.4. Complete panic sequence.

Background Information

Rosemary is a 32-year-old emergency room nurse who is now in her third year of marriage. She has worked as a nurse in emergency medicine for approximately 11 years and has just recently begun to plan a family with her husband.

Approximately one month ago, Rosemary began experiencing what she describes as frightening feelings while driving home from work. Initially, she shrugged the experience off as being "wound up from work," but after it occurred a second and third time, she became concerned. She underwent a complete medical evaluation with her family physician and also consulted a cardiologist on her own accord. All test results were unremarkable, and it was therefore suggested that she consult a mental health professional for stress management.

Rosemary's family physician referred her for an initial evaluation, at which time a full clinical history was conducted, along with the administration of the Structural Clinical Interview Schedule for DSM-III-R (SCID). The scale yielded a differential diagnosis of panic disorder on Axis 1 with no diagnosis on Axis II or III. There were no unusual stressors that precipitated her anxiety other than those associated with her work. She had no other history of emotional or behavioral problems including drug or alcohol use. She was administered the Beck Anxiety Inventory (BAI) (Beck, 1987), which yielded a score of 28 (severe), as well as the Beck Depression Inventory (BDI) (Beck, Ward, Mendelson, Mock, & Erbaugh, 1961), which produced a score of 11 (mild).

Rosemary reports that her marriage is happy and she is content with her life. She has been feeling some stress with regard to her career over the past two years and has had thoughts of resigning or transferring to another branch of medicine. The dialogue below took place in the first session after the two session intake.

Case Vignette

Therapist: *Rosemary, how are you feeling today?*
Rosemary: *Well, not so good. I had another bad week again with panic attacks galore! Now I know that we only conducted the intake so far, but Doctor I just can't take much more of this* (begins to sob). *And now that I just found that I am pregnant, I can't even resort to the lorazepam that my family doctor gave me.*
Therapist: *Okay, Rosemary, I sense the urgency and want to get started immediately with the treatment phase; however, we need to spend just a bit more time attempting to conceptualize your panic sequence and trying to make sense of how the panic cycle escalates within you. This is very important as we begin to design the specific treatment intervention. So, if you can just bear with me a bit longer.*
Rosemary: *Fine—So let's get moving with this because it's beginning to take its toll on me.*
Therapist: *All right! Now, you stated to me during the last session*

*that these attacks appear to occur "out of the blue" with no precipi-
tating event.*

Rosemary: *Yes, it's so strange, almost like I am going into "V-tac"*
(ventricular tachycardia). *But of course I know I am not, or at least I
don't think that I am.*

Therapist: *Well, you have already been thoroughly evaluated by a cardiologist and you are fine cardiovascularly, so it's the spontaneity of
these attacks that takes you by surprise, correct?*

Rosemary: *Yes! They seem to overpower me, but I know that it's
nothing really serious and I feel so stupid sitting here telling you this.*

Therapist: *Well, I can understand how you feel, many people in your
position experience this. What we need to do is identify what symptoms typically trigger your panic sequence. Is there any one or two
symptoms that you experience initially? Can you recall?*

Rosemary: *Oh boy. Ah, let me see . . . I don't know, it's sort of a thing
that takes me by surprise. It just comes on, and I feel overwhelmed.*

Therapist: *Okay, but try to focus on what you experience first. For
example, let's focus on your most recent panic attack.*

Rosemary: *Well, that was two days ago.*

Therapist: *Where were you? What happened?*

Rosemary: *I was driving home from my 7:30 to 3:30 shift, and I had
an attack in the car again.*

Therapist: *All right, now I would like you to just close your eyes for a
moment and try to imagine yourself back in your car driving home
from work yesterday just prior to the onset of the attack. Can you recall at what point you had the onset of the attack.*

Rosemary: *Yes, Okay. I remember now, it was in front of the Acme
store. It started with my heart, or at least that was one of the early
symptoms that really alarmed me, but I am not so sure.*

Therapist: *Okay, and then what symptoms followed that, can you recall?*

Rosemary: *Well, I know somewhere close to that I had shortness of
breath.*

Therapist: *But you're not really sure?*

Rosemary: *No, I guess I just kind of blocked it out somehow like I
always do because it's so overwhelming to me. You know, this may
sound odd, but I wish that I could almost experience a panic attack
right now, just so you could see what I go through during these attacks.*

Therapist: *Well, there is an exercise that is designed to do just that,
not perhaps to the extent that you might experience symptoms during
a spontaneous attack, but close maybe.*

Rosemary: *Oh great! Now I am sorry I mentioned anything about it!*
Therapist: *Well, look, we don't have to do that, but I thought that I might mention it to you because it has been successful in helping some panic sufferers identify their symptoms and their adjoining thoughts and reactions.*
Rosemary: *Well, I don't know. I mean, it sounds like it may help, but I am not exactly keen on giving myself a panic attack right now.*
Therapist: *Well, you see, that's the point; the idea here is that in reality you may just be doing that more than you are aware of. Perhaps many of your attacks are brought on by the manner in which you catastrophically misinterpret bodily sensations—in this case, heart palpitations, lightheadedness, and so on. Therefore, it is very important that we try to identify and pinpoint this sequence so that we can then devise a plan for intervention.*
Rosemary: *Well, okay. I'll give it a try, you're the doctor, if you think it will help. Just so that this doesn't make me worse. I mean, I know that I can't die from this or anything, but sometimes I just feel like I am going to, do you know what I mean?*
Therapist: *No, you won't die from it. We've already had you checked out thoroughly through Dr. Bleam, your family physician, as well as your cardiologist. Remember, he did the electrocardiogram on your heart and all that blood work that you enjoyed so much.*
Rosemary: *Yeah, I remember, and everything came back NORMAL.*
(It is essential, prior to this exercise, that medical clearance be obtained through a physician to insure that the patient does not have any significant cardiovascular disorder [coronary artery disease, arrhythmia] or a seizure disorder, etc.)
Therapist: *Right, so let's give it a try!*
Rosemary: *Okay, what do I have to do?*
Therapist: *I would like you to begin to breathe in a special way in inhaling and exhaling only through your mouth, very quickly almost as you would if you were out of breath, like this* (therapist demonstrates method of breathing). *All right. Now you try it along with me—short staccato-type breaths.* (Rosemary mimics the same procedure.)
Therapist: *Great! Now let's try it for real. I am going to say "go" and I want you to begin breathing along with me in the manner that we just attempted. Once we start, I am going to discontinue, but I want you to continue on for about . . . oh, maybe 1-1/2 to 2 minutes for as long as you can, nonstop. I have a glass of water here since your mouth may become dry. Okay? Are you ready?*
Rosemary: *Yes, I guess!*
Therapist: *Let's begin.* (Therapist and Rosemary begin the exercise

together. Throughout the exercise, the therapist supports Rosemary in her breathing by doing it with her simultaneously for short periods of time and keeps track of the time.)

Rosemary: (Only 45 seconds into the exercise, breathing very heavily) *I can't do this anymore! My heart is starting to race like crazy.*

Therapist: *Okay, what are you feeling right now?*

Rosemary: *Well, I don't like not being able to breath real well; I sort of enjoy breathing!*

Therapist: *What's going through your mind as you say that to me and experience these sensations?*

Rosemary: *I am thinking to myself, I am going to have one of those attacks, it never fails, I just don't trust my body, I want to leave, run away.*

Therapist: *Let's try to go just a little further with the breathing to see if you experience any other symptoms.*

Rosemary: *Sure, whatever you say. You're the doctor.*

Therapist: *Rosemary, try to remember that this is a diagnostic test designed to help both of us learn to control your panic. It's not meant to give you a hard time.*

Rosemary: *I know, I just hate having these damn attacks!* (Rosemary resumes the breathing exercise.)

Rosemary: (As another 50 seconds passes) *Oh no! I have to stop. I'm getting worse.* (Begins to cry) *I didn't want to do this because of what might happen.*

Therapist: *Okay, just try to calm down and tell me what's happening.*

Rosemary: *Dr. Dattilio help me, please! I feel like I am out of control.*

Therapist: *What are you experiencing, Rosemary?*

Rosemary: *I am having lightheadedness and tingling in my hands . . . they feel numb . . . oh God, I hate this! What's wrong with me? I am losing it!* (crying)

Therapist: *All right, Rosemary, just begin to breathe slowly with me now. Let's calm ourselves down. Close your eyes and just breathe slowly and continuously, inhaling slowly through the nose and exhaling slowly through the mouth so that we slow everything back down to your normal resting state.* (Several minutes pass as Rosemary does this.)

Therapist: *How do you feel now?*

Rosemary: *Better, but still a little dazed, like I'm in a fog.*

Therapist: *All right, well, that should pass in a little while. Let's talk about the experience that you just had while it is fresh in your mind.*

Rosemary: *I didn't like it. It was almost as bad as what I had in the car the other day.*

Therapist: *Well, actually that's kind of good, because it provides us with some insight into what you experience during an attack. So, let's try to reconstruct what just went on with you and see whether or not there is some connection to what occurs each time you experience an attack.*

Rosemary: *So, we're just going to talk, no more breathing?*

Therapist: *Yes, no more breathing, at least for now! Now, when we first began the exercise, you stated that you felt your "heart pounding."*

Rosemary: *Correct!*

Therapist: *So, is it fair to say that this is usually the initial symptom?*

Rosemary: *Yes.*

Therapist: *All right now, do you remember a few minutes ago when we began doing the exercise and your heart rate began to increase?*

Rosemary: *Yes.*

Therapist: *What thoughts went racing through your mind at that point?*

Rosemary: *Probably "What's going on? What's happening?"*

Therapist: *Okay, and then do you remember what you felt . . . or did?*

Rosemary: *Well, I began to really worry.*

Therapist: *Great, so we have the initial sequence of what occurred with you during the fist few seconds of the attack. Let's get this down on paper.* (See Figure 3.2.)

Therapist: *So what do you think so far, does this look accurate to you?*

Rosemary: *Yes, very accurate. The more that I think about it, that's exactly what has been happening to me each time.*

Therapist: *Okay then, let's continue. So next, we have what?*

Rosemary: *Ah, I am not really sure.* (It is not uncommon for patients to block on recalling these symptoms, even after the use of the panic induction exercise. This is primarily due to the aversiveness of the sensations and the catastrophic thought content associated with them.)

Therapist: *Well, let's go back and look at those Beck Anxiety Inventories that you filled out and also what we have captured on paper during the panic induction. All right, we have marked here, "Increase and difficulty in breathing" and "Lightheadedness and sweating." Do you agree?*

Rosemary: *Yes, this seems right.*

Therapist: *Okay, now we need to attach the thought and emotion-slash-behavior to each of these.*

The process then is continued all the way through to the last symptom that Rosemary can recall experiencing, which in this case is a tingling in the hands and feet. Vectors are then drawn from these last symptoms to all aforementioned symptoms, automatic thoughts, and emotions/behaviors to depict a continuous cycle portrayed in Figure 3.4.

As can be observed, this figure depicts the escalation process of the panic cycle in this particular case involving cognitions and affect as well as behaviors. The connection is demonstrated via the vectors drawn. Vectors are also drawn downward from each sensation in order to indicate the sympathetic chain that occurs autonomically in this process aside from the escalation caused by thoughts, emotion, and behaviors.

This has a number of therapeutic effects aside from allowing the panic sufferer to see the sequence of events graphically. It also allows for the individual breakdown of each symptom so that the patient and therapist can both intervene at various levels, particularly when attempting to restructure specific catastrophic misinterpretation. It may also be easier for the therapist and patient to collaboratively rewrite new cognitive interpretations and substitute alternative emotions and behaviors.

It is hoped that this case vignette provides readers with an adequate description of how the SAEB technique and conceptualization process would be implemented with patients. The beauty of this system is that it can be used continually throughout the treatment process to aid patients in monitoring their cognitions, affect, and behavior in response to physiological sensations. Patients can recall the process each time they reexperience bodily sensations that appear to be threatening. This method can be used virtually at any point in the treatment continuum and requires very little coaching subsequent to the initial introduction. Patients are usually encouraged to use this system outside of the therapy hour, particularly during panic-prone periods or high-stress events (Dattilio & Kendall, in press). It is important that patients are able to conceptualize how they are over-responding to bodily sensations that may be normal reactions to life stress and catastrophically misinterpreting these sensations as dangerous so that they trigger an escalated state of panic.

Although panic induction may be an appropriate and effective way of eliciting the SAEB progression with many patients suffering with panic and possibly other types of anxiety disorders, for some it may not be advisable. Patients with any cardiovascular difficulties or seizure-related disorders should not try panic induction because of the potential physiological stress of the exercise. Also, aside from any medical preclusions, much of the effectiveness of the symptom induction exercise may depend on the patient's ability to sustain such a vigorous exercise and the courage to reexperience an actual panic attack or a close approximation. In addition, panic sufferers who experience atypical panic attacks or whose sensations are subdued by virtue of the use of anxiolytic or antidepressant compounds may not achieve good results with the panic induction exercise. If patients possess good recall and are able to simulate or reexperience panic sensations without the use of the symptom induction technique, then the SAEB system may still be useful as a method of conceptualization.

Summary

Individuals suffering from panic attacks are often at a loss as to explain what they experience during an episode of panic. Their thoughts, emotions, and behaviors often blend with the physical sensations, creating an overwhelming and sometimes incapacitating terror that words seem inadequate to describe.

The SAEB system is designed to aid panic victims by providing a structure for outlining their experience in all of these domains (cognitive, emotional, behavioral, and physiological) so that it becomes less of an enigma to them, reducing some of the debilitation as well as the frustration.

In summary, the SAEB system may be used with most persons who experience panic. It is recommended that clinicians first attempt to gather background information pertinent to anxiety and symptoms similarly experienced in the past. Next, it is important that the patient undergo the necessary medical clearance that will allow for an induction exercise to be utilized (i.e., rule out cardiovascular disease, seizure disorders, and other relevant conditions). Once this is achieved, then the therapist should make an attempt to ascertain the sequence of symptoms that are experienced at the onset and during the panic episode. The therapist can then align these with any associated or concurrent thoughts, emotions, and behaviors.

Although the SAEB system is simple and straightforward to apply, it is nonetheless a highly structured and focused technique for aiding individuals to better conceptualize the onset of their panic attacks and a strategy for controlling and eventually diminishing their heightened levels of anxiety. In conjunction with other established intervention techniques such as exposure, the SAEB system can be a valuable tool in the treatment of panic attacks.

References

Alford, B. A., Beck, A. T., Freeman, A., & Wright, F. (1990). Brief focused cognitive therapy of panic disorder. *Psychotherapy, 27*(2), 230-234.

Barlow, D. H. (1988). *Anxiety and its disorders.* New York: Guilford.

Beck, A. T. (1987). *Anxiety inventory.* Philadelphia: Center for Cognitive Therapy.

Beck, A. T., Emery, G., & Greenberg, R. L. (1985). *Anxiety disorders and phobias: A cognitive perspective.* New York: Basic Books.

Beck A. T., Solkol, L., Clark, D. A., Berchick, R., & Wright, F. (1992). A crossover study of focused cognitive therapy for panic disorder. *American Journal of Psychiatry, 149*(6), 778-783.

Beck, A. T., Ward, C. H., Mendelson, M., Mock, J. E., & Erbaugh, J. K. (1961). An inventory for measuring depression. *Archives of General Psychiatry, 4,* 561-571.

Weekly panic log. Center for Cognitive Therapy, The Science Center, Room 754, 36009 Market Street, Philadelphia, PA.

Chambless, D. L., Caputo, G. C., Bright, P., & Gallagher, R. (1984). Assessment of fear of fear in agoraphobia: The Body Sensations Questionnaire and The Agoraphobic Questionnaire. *Journal of Consulting & Clinical Psychology, 52,* 1090-1097.

Clark, D. M. (1986). A cognitive approach to panic. *Behaviour Research and Therapy, 24,* 461-471.

Craske, M. G., & Barlow, D. H. (1993). Panic disorder and agoraphobia. In D. H. Barlow (Ed.), *Clinical handbook of psychological disorders* (3rd ed.) (pp. 1-47). New York: Guilford.

Dattilio, F. M. (1986). Differences in cognitive responses to fear among individuals diagnosed as panic disorder, generalized anxiety disorder, agoraphobia with panic attacks and simple phobia (doctoral dissertation, Temple University). *Dissertation Abstracts International, 48,* O3A.

Dattilio, F. M. (1992a). Interoceptive sensations during sexual arousal and panic. *The Behavior Therapist, 15*(9), 231-233.

Dattilio, F. M. (1992b). *The SAEB System: Crisis intervention techniques with panic.* Symposium on crisis intervention presented at the 26th Annual Association for Advancement of Behavior Therapy (AABT), Boston, MA.

Dattilio, F. M. (1994a). Paradoxical intention as an alternative in the treatment of panic attacks. *Journal of Cognitive Psychotherapy, 8*(1), 33-40.

Dattilio, F. M. (1994b). *The SAEB system and symptom induction in the treatment of panic* (videotape). Bristol, PA: Taylor & Francis.

Dattilio, F. M., & Berchick, R. J. (1992). Panic with agoraphobia. In A. Freeman & F. M. Dattilio (Eds.), *Comprehensive casebook of cognitive therapy* (pp. 89-98). New York: Plenum.

Dattilio, F. M., & Kendall, P. C. (1994). Cognitive-behavioral strategies: Applications to panic disorder in crisis intervention. In F. M. Dattilio & A. Freeman (Eds.), *Cognitive-behavioral approaches to crisis intervention.* New York: Guilford.

Ehlers, A. (1993). Somatic symptoms and panic attacks: A retrospective study of learning experiences. *Behaviour Research and Therapy, 31*(3), 269-278.

Greenberg, R. L. (1989). Panic disorder and agoraphobia. In J. Scott, J. M. G. Williams, & A. T. Beck (Eds.), *Cognitive therapy in clinical practice: An illustrative casebook* (pp. 25-40). London: Routledge and Kegan Paul.

Klosko, J. S., Barlow, D. H., Tassinari, R., & Cerny, J. A. (1990). A comparison of alprozalam and behavior therapy in the treatment of panic disorder. *Journal of Consulting and Clinical Psychology, 58,* 77-84.

Michelson, L., Marchione, K., Greenwald, M., Glanz, L., Testa, S., & Marchione, N. (1990). Panic disorder: Cognitive-behavioral treatment. *Behaviour Research and Therapy, 28,* 141-151.

Ottaviani, R., & Beck, A. T. (1987). Cognitive aspects of panic disorders. *Journal of Anxiety Disorders, 1,* 15-28.

Sanderson, W. C., & Wetzler, S. (1993). Observations on the cognitive behavioral treatment of panic disorder: Impact of benzodiasepines. *Psychotherapy, 30*(1), 125-132.

Solkol, L., Beck, A. T., Greenberg, R. L., Wright, F. D., & Berchick, R. J. (1989). Cognitive therapy of panic disorder: A nonpharmacological alternative. *Journal of Nervous and Mental Disease, 177,* 711-716.

Wolpe, J., & Rowan, V. (1988). Panic disorder: A product of classical conditioning. *Behaviour Research and Therapy, 26,* 441-450.

VIGOROUS DISPUTING OF IRRATIONAL BELIEFS IN RATIONAL-EMOTIVE BEHAVIOR THERAPY (REBT)

Therapist: Albert Ellis, Ph.D.

Affiliation: Psychologist, Executive Director, Institute for Rational-Emotive Therapy

Major works:

> Ellis, A. (1988). *How to stubbornly refuse to make yourself miserable about anything—yes anything!* Secaurus, NJ: Lyle Stuart.
>
> Ellis, A. (1988). *Reason and emotion in psychotherapy* (revised ed.). New York: Carol Publishing Group.
>
> Ellis, A. (1995). *Better, deeper, and more enduring brief therapy.* New York: Brunner-Mazel
>
> Author or editor of over 50 books and monographs, as well as over 500 journal articles, Ellis is the founding father of Rational-Emotive Behavior Therapy.

Population for whom the technique is appropriate: No restrictions.

Cautionary notes: None.

Explain to clients what rational (self-help) and irrational (self-defeating) beliefs are in REBT and how they can discover and dispute their irrational beliefs (IB's) empirically, logically, and pragmatically. Explain that they easily can hold Rational Beliefs (RB's) lightly and weakly while still holding—and devoutly believing—IB's strongly and forcefully. Thus, they can lightly believe, "I want people to like me and can live happily if they don't" and much more powerfully believe, "But I really absolutely need their approval and have nothing to live for if I don't get it!" Their REBT disputing of their IB's, therefore, had often better be very vigorous, forceful, and persistent, until they thoroughly change the IB's and actually replace them with RB's.

You can explain this to your clients, show them how to do vigorous REBT disputing, and encourage them to often do it as a homework assignment. Thus, you can give clients these written instructions:

> One way to do highly powerful, vigorous disputing is to use a tape recorder and to record one of your strong Irrational Beliefs into it,

such as, "If I fail this job interview I am about to have, that will prove that I'll never get a good job and that I might as well apply only for low-level positions!" Figure out several Disputes to this IB and *strongly* present them on this same tape. For example: "Even if I do poorly on this interview, that only will show that I failed *this* time, but never will show that I'll *always* fail and can *never* do well in *other* interviews. Maybe they'll still hire me for the job. But if they don't, I can learn by my mistakes, can do better in other interviews, and likely can get the kind of job that I want."

Listen to your Disputing. Let other people, including your therapist or members of your therapy group, listen to it. Do it over in a more forceful and vigorous manner and let them listen to it again, to see if you do it better and more forcefully, until they agree that you are getting more powerful at doing it. Keep listening to it until you see that you are able to convince yourself and others that your Disputing is becoming more and more powerful and more convincing.

Keep after your clients to do this kind of vigorous REBT disputing and to let you (and members of their group) listen to it, critique it, and show them how to master this technique. If you keep vigorously—but undamningly—after them, they may keep vigorously after their own Irrational Beliefs!

This technique will work well with many clients who dispute weakly and lightly. When, somehow, it does not seem to be working, investigate other IB's that clients are not disputing and consider using several of REBT's other emotive-evocative methods as well. Suggestions include (a) rational emotive imagery and (b) role reversal, where you (or someone else) rigidly hold to a client's Irrational Beliefs and the client vigorously talks you out of these (his or her own) IB's.

ART THERAPY

Therapist: Phoebe Farris-Dufrene, Ph.D.

Affiliation: Registered Art Therapist; National Certified Counselor; Licensed Clinical Social Worker (Indiana); Purdue University; private practice.

Major works:
> Coleman, V. D., & Farris-Dufrene, P. (1996). *Art therapy and psychotherapy: Blending two therapeutic approaches*. Muncie, IN: Accelerated Development.
>
> Author of a book on Native American artists; 20 articles in art therapy, art education, and counseling; and essays for three books and encyclopedias.

Population for whom the technique is appropriate: Children, adolescents, and adults in individual, group, and family sessions.

Cautionary notes: As with any therapeutic modality or technique, art therapy should be practiced only by clinicians who have been well-trained in an accredited institution; are certified, licensed, or registered in that discipline; and are involved in ongoing supervision and/or continuing education during their professional career. For the field of art therapy, the American Art Therapy Association is the national organization involved with registration/certification, the establishment of accreditation guidelines for training institutions, and publication of a scholarly quarterly developed for art therapy. Clients seeking art therapy services should feel free to question prospective art therapists about their qualifications.

Since the 1970s, art therapy has rapidly become a part of the academic milieu. Colleges and universities are offering courses, and entire therapy training programs are being developed in many parts of the country (Wadeson, 1989). More than 20 universities and colleges presently offer art therapy courses as part of their art education program. This is in addition to specialized graduate degree programs in art therapy (American Art Therapy Association [AATA], 1989). For art educators, counselors, etc. interested in utilizing their knowledge of media techniques, visual symbol production, and other intrinsic facets of the art experience toward therapeutic aims, an understanding of art therapy is essential.

Art therapy recognizes art processes, forms, content, and associations as reflections of an individual's development, abilities, personality, interests, and concerns. Art as therapy implies that the creative process can be a means both of reconciling emotional conflicts and of fostering self-awareness and personal growth. It may be used in treatment, assessment, and evaluation (AATA, 1989). Through observation and analysis of art behaviors, art products, and the client's communications, the art therapist/art educator for the handicapped formulates diagnostic assessments, treatment, rehabilitation, and remediation plans. Because art is a universal language of humankind, the expressive modality of art therapy can be utilized by clients from widely divergent countries, cultures, and ethnic backgrounds to exchange feelings, moods, ideas, and thoughts in a non-threatening, non-verbal manner.

Art therapy educators such as Kramer and Wilson (1979) have recognized that art and the creative process involves a complex comprehension both of the physical handling of art materials in order to form them so that they serve as symbolic equivalents for human experience and of the psychic processes that motivate creative work. Understanding of these ideas about the nature of art is necessary to understand the function of art as therapy. The art therapist must recognize and respond to the hidden as well as the overt aspects of the client's production.

Art therapy involves practical and theoretical considerations involved in therapeutic art, developmental theory, artistic development, cognitive development, perception, and affective uses in the context of art and psychodynamic processes. Populations served include the emotionally disturbed, mentally retarded, learning disabled, physically disabled, and others. Institutions providing art therapy include but are not limited to special education schools, psychiatric hospitals, outpatient mental health clinics, rehabilitation centers, prisons, and private psychotherapy firms.

Increasingly, art therapy as practiced in the United States and Europe is spreading to other countries around the world and being adapted to their indigenous, cultural needs. The author has conducted research on art therapy in Mexico, Cuba, and Brazil. Because of the use of the arts for healing among indigenous peoples since ancient times, art therapy is also effective for contemporary indigenous peoples such as Native Americans who often embrace both traditional and Western lifestyles. The author, of Powhatan descent, is also active in researching and practicing traditional uses of the arts for healing in Native American cultures.

Although this author has ambivalent feelings about the use of the term "techniques," some of the art therapy practices or "techniques" commonly used are the following: drawing, painting, or sculpting self-portraits or family portraits;

drawing, painting, or sculpting dreams, fears, and fantasies; visually creating traumatic experiences such as physical or sexual abuse; visually creating free-forms of self-expression (abstract or representational); projective drawing techniques such as the D-A-P (Draw a Person), H-T-P (House, Tree, Person), K-F-D (Kinetic Family Drawing); and newer drawing assessments developed by art therapists.

The use of art, combined with psychotherapy, in the healing process is gaining widespread popularity. The range of art forms being utilized also can be broadened. Jennings (1990) promoted drama therapy, which emphasizes the art form of drama and theater as its central focus as a clinical and educational approach to gaining personal insight. Movement, art, and drama have been reported to bring about substantive gains in therapy when body image issues are being addressed, and masks and videos have been used to facilitate interpersonal communication. Music also has been combined with other creative modalities in treatments.

Art therapy is being used for an increasing range of experiences and with all age groups. Art has proven to be an important aid in the treatment of relationship problems. Art therapy is an appropriate and effective way to evaluate and treat physically and sexually abused children. Young victims often can express their feelings about abuse more easily through art. Art therapy also enables them to be more assertive and self-protective in both sexual and non-sexual situations (Hagood, 1991).

Therapists have found that post-session art making is useful for processing strong feelings or giving form to unacknowledged feelings brought about by the interaction with clients (Wadeson, 1989). Useful clinical information may be provided and empathy may increase with the therapist's use of post-session art.

Artistic creations sometimes reveal facets of personality not easily accessible through verbal psychotherapy. Important diagnostic indications may be discussed through free art expression before they can be identified by more conventional projective techniques. Symbolic content and the formal characteristics of the work constitute a source of information uniquely available through the visual arts.

References

American Art Therapy Association. (1989). *Art therapy guidelines and practices*. Mundelein, IL: Author.

Hagood, M. (1991). Group art therapy with mothers of sexually abused children. *The Arts in Psychotherapy, 18,* 17-27.

Jennings, S. (1990). *Dramatherapy with families, groups, and individuals: Waiting in the wings.* London: J. Kingsley.

Kramer, E., & Wilson, L. (1979). *Childhood and art therapy: Notes on theory and application.* New York: Schocken Books.

Wadeson, H. (1989). *Advances in art therapy.* Springfield, IL: Charles C. Thomas.

VOICE THERAPY

Therapist: Robert W. Firestone, Ph.D.

Affiliation: Clinical psychologist and author, The Glendon Association, Santa Barbara, California.

Major works:
>   Firestone, R. W. (1985). The fantasy bond: Structure of psychological defenses. New York: Human Sciences Press.
>   Firestone, R. W. (1990). *Compassionate child-rearing: An approach to optimal parenting.* New York: Insight Books, Plenum Press.
>   Firestone, R. W. (1997). *Combating destructive thought processes: Voice therapy and separation theory,* Thousand Oaks, CA: Sage Publications.
>   Author of audio-visual mental health training materials and the *Firestone Assessment of Self-destructive Thoughts (FAST)* test, which discriminates suicidal from nonsuicidal patients.

Population for whom the technique is appropriate: The methods can be applied in individual and group treatment of depression and various forms of self-destructive behaviors including addiction; to interventions with patients at risk for suicide and violent behavior; and in couples therapy and parent education.

Cautionary notes: None.

My theoretical approach represents a broadly based system of concepts and hypotheses that integrate psychoanalytic and existential frameworks, yet should not be considered eclectic. The theory on which voice therapy is based explains how early trauma leads to defense formation and how these original defenses are reinforced as the child gradually becomes aware of his or her own mortality.

The explanatory principle that I term the "voice" represents the language of the defensive process. It may be defined as an organized system of internalized thoughts and associated affects alien or hostile to a person's self-interest. Negative thought processes, or voices, are made up of conscious and unconscious components that obstruct the ongoing motivational field and cause varying degrees of maladjustment.

The therapeutic methodology to which the concept of the voice has been applied is an affective-cognitive therapy. The purpose of voice therapy is to separate and bring out into the open elements of the personality that are antithetical to self resulting from the internalization of negative parental attitudes and damaging childhood experiences. The emphasis on exposing negative thought processes in my work overlaps cognitive theories and therapies to a certain extent, yet my approach is very different in that the methods deal more with the expression of feeling than analysis of logic or illogic. The expression of affect that often accompanies the verbalization of the voice leads to unusual insights.

Voice therapy was originally a laboratory procedure used to understand personality dynamics and only secondarily evolved into a psychotherapeutic methodology. The model of psychotherapy that has evolved was the basis for an instrument to assess suicide potential and other self-destructive behavior and has been validated with over 1,300 outpatient and inpatient subjects. The instrument that was developed, *The Firestone Assessment of Self-destructive Thoughts,* was found to distinguish suicidal from nonsuicidal subjects more accurately than other instruments. Recently, a new scale, the *Firestone Voice Scale for Violence* was developed, based on the same theory of psychopathology and in a sample of 916 subjects, distinguished incarcerated subjects, parolees, and participants in anger management groups from nonviolent subjects.

When used as a therapeutic procedure, the specialized techniques of voice therapy consist of three components: (a) the process of eliciting and identifying negative thought patterns, rendering them more accessible and susceptible to control; (b) the feeling release component—recovering repressed emotions and releasing the affect associated with destructive thinking; and (c) counteracting self-destructive behaviors regulated by the voice through the collaborative planning and application of appropriate corrective experiences. It is important to emphasize that these components are not necessarily undertaken in the order delineated here.

In the first phase of treatment, patients learn to verbalize their self-critical, self-destructive thoughts in the second person, as though another person were addressing them—that is, in the form of statements toward themselves rather than statements about themselves. An example would be, "You're worthless. You don't matter to anybody," rather than "I feel like I'm a worthless person. I really don't matter to anybody." Expressing the voice in this format facilitates the process of separating the patient's own point of view from alien, hostile thought patterns assimilated during the developmental stages. The process of identifying the voice can be approached intellectually as an analytical or cognitive technique, or more dramatically using cathartic methods.

To clarify the specific technique for verbalizing the voice, the patient presents a problem. For example, he or she complains about the onset of depression. The therapist might ask, "When did you start feeling this way?" The patient describes an event that he or she believes signaled the onset of the problem. The therapist inquires, "What do you think you were telling yourself about this event?" The patient discusses his or her thoughts related to the event. If, for instance, the incident was a phone call, where a male patient asked for a date and was rejected, the therapist asks, "What were you telling yourself about being turned down?"

The patient at this point might say, "I was telling myself that I'm not very attractive. I'm not very interesting. Girls don't like me very much." The therapist then instructs the patient to say these thoughts in the second person, as a voice, for example, "*You're* not attractive. *You're* not interesting. No girl would like *you.*" When the patient puts his or her thoughts in this form, strong feelings emerge, and the whole affective tone of the verbalization is transformed from flat, mater-of-fact statements to an intense emotional outpouring. As patients express the voice in this format, they usually have their own steam and keep the words and feelings going on their own volition. The therapist simply offers encouragement with statements like, "Say it louder." "Don't hold back."

Although it is relatively easy to elicit the destructive voice process and bring it to the surface, voice therapy is not a short-term procedure or a simple cure-all. It is impossible to conceive of "cure" without the patient being able to change the fundamental aspects of the way he or she is living out his or her defensive structure. Voice therapy is a serious approach, requiring a strong clinician who is familiar with the underlying theory and who, ideally, is relatively free of his or her own defenses or defensiveness. The techniques outlined here, albeit governed by the patient's level of ego strength, allow for behavioral changes that often go beyond what is possible in many other therapeutic formats. Because individuals in voice therapy are engaged in breaking with powerful defenses that have limited and depleted their energy, it is vital that the therapeutic approach offer maximum opportunity for emancipation and expansion of personal boundaries.

References

Firestone, R. W. (1985). *The fantasy bond: Structure of psychological defenses.* New York: Human Sciences Press.

Firestone, R. W. (1988). *Voice therapy: A psychotherapeutic approach to self-destructive behavior.* New York: Human Sciences Press.

Firestone, R. W. (1990). *Compassionate child-rearing: An approach to optimal parenting.* New York: Insight Books, Plenum Press.

Firestone, R. W. (1997). *Combating destructive thought processes: Voice therapy and separation theory.* Newbury Park, CA: Sage Publications.

Firestone, R. W. (in press). *The inner voice in suicide: Assessment, treatment, and case management.* Newbury Park, CA: Sage Publications.

Firestone, R. W., & Firestone, L. A. (1996). *Manual for the Firestone Assessment of Self-destructive Thoughts.* San Antonio, TX: The Psychological Corporation.

WORKING FROM CLIENT EXPERIENTIAL VIGNETTES

Therapist: Sterling K. Gerber, Ph.D.

Affiliation: Washington Certified Counselor; ABPP Diplomate in Counseling Psychology; Counselor Educator, Eastern Washington University.

Major work:
> Gerber, S. K. (1986). *Responsive therapy: A systematic approach to counseling skills.* New York: Human Sciences Press.

Population for whom the technique is appropriate: Appropriate for clients above age 10 who have relatively intact ego function.

Cautionary notes: None.

There are several ways of typifying the therapeutic process. One suggests that therapy proceeds through four stages: ventilation, clarification, alteration, and accommodation. This approach is centered in the clarification phase. Following whatever ventilation is necessary for the client to begin focused disclosure, the therapist uses a series of techniques intended to seek free client disclosure of progressively specific experiential examples. The intent is to arrive at a mutual awareness between client and therapist of client circumstance and style. By circumstance is meant the problem dynamics being faced and the resources readily available to the client. By style is meant the preferred and customary method by which the client engages in problem solving.

This differs from much "talk therapy" in that it de-emphasizes client cognitive conclusions and the difficulties in communication of such in favor of client descriptions of experience, which are closer to primary data disclosure than that which the client has processed cognitively. Simply, the counselor directs the client to give specific and complete examples of what is going on and of how the client is responding.

The process begins with a direction to the client to disclose, such as, "Tell me what it's like being you," or "Talk to me about you." Whatever the client discloses is responded to by therapist paraphrase or reflection. This establishes the necessary process wherein client discloses, counselor understands. Questioning is avoided intentionally and religiously. The insertion of a question by the therapist tends to change the dynamics such that the client will not disclose freely; he or she will, instead, try to give what is requested. This means the focus has shifted from the client's phenomenal sphere over to the counselor's. A second problem of questions is that they tend to disrupt the free flow of client disclosure.

Client disclosure is facilitated by counselor directions to, "Give me an example," and, "Be more specific." As the client produces experiential vignettes, the therapist acts as a mirror, giving reflection back to the client of precisely stated content, denotative labels for feelings, and "bottom line" statements of message, and even cautiously speaking for the client some of the things obvious in the example and not yet verbalized by the client. It must be understood that these reflections are perceptually based and do not come from the counselor's cognitive analysis. As the counselor puts himself or herself into the experience being described by the client, it is possible to experience vicariously the client's position and verbalize some of those vicarious experiences.

As the therapist helps the client process through several examples, it is possible for the therapist to see patterns and to draw his or her own conclusions regarding the dynamics thus exposed. An example might be something such as this: after the client shares anecdotes of how several different members of his family repeatedly sought him out to confide problems, individual and in relation one to another, he makes statements such as, "I can't understand why they are the way they are. I've racked my brain trying to figure out something to say to them to resolve these petty issues." The counselor sees a circumstance wherein the client is hooked into a neurotic pattern of interactions with his family members (a behavioral problem being perpetuated by external contingencies) and insists on solving the problem by thinking about it (a cognitive style). The therapist says something such as, "It's your job to fix your family and you don't know how to do it."

Admittedly this is a greatly oversimplified example, yet it includes most of the critical dynamics. Clients typically respond at this juncture with one of two classes of response. They often reframe for themselves when confronted with the clarified perception and use an alternative and obvious solution such as, "No. It really isn't my job. I don't have to go through this anymore. Nobody is chaining me to my chair when they start dumping. I can tell them I choose not to be involved this time; they can work it out themselves." In this event, therapy is over. The client can move under his own initiative to solve his problem in his newly perceived manner.

The other class of response is something such as, "You're right. I don't know how to get out of this defeating pattern. Help me." In this event, the therapist and the client move into the third phase of therapy, the alteration phase, wherein the therapist takes an active role in teaching, directing, or conditioning the client to a self-enhancing response.

A frequent conclusion for therapists in response to clients is, "What you're doing isn't working." This perceptual approach, usually accomplished within the initial three sessions of therapy, is a systematic way to describe (a) the dynamics of the situation in which the client exists (the circumstance), (b) the unsuccessful attempts at solution already manifested by the client (the style), and (c) the desired and so far elusive state of acceptable resolution. The statement, attributed to Rollo May, that "Technique follows understanding," is an appropriate conclusion to this method. Gaining a clear understanding of the circumstance and style is a direct and logical step to selecting or creating an intervention that has a high probability of success, so direct and logical that the client often can do it for himself or herself.

REALITY THERAPY AND CHOICE THEORY

Therapist: William Glasser, M.D.

Affiliation: Psychiatrist, private practice; Director of the William Glasser Institute, Chatsworth, California; founding father of Reality Therapy.

Major works:
Glasser, W. (1965). *Reality therapy.* New York: HarperCollins.
Glasser, W. (1984). *Control theory.* New York: HarperCollins.
Glasser, W. (1985). *Staying together.* New York: HarperCollins.

Cautionary notes: None.

I have been practicing and teaching *Reality Therapy* since 1962. Its basic premise remains the same as when I began: *we are responsible for what we do and we choose all we do.* But as the years have gone by, I have developed a psychological theory, *Choice Theory*, that explains in great detail how we function. This theory is now not only the theoretical basis for reality therapy but also an integral part of the therapy itself. A skilled practitioner of reality therapy will try to teach choice theory to the client, and the only way the practitioner can learn to do this well is to put this theory to work in every part of his or her own life.

While it is impossible to explain all of choice theory in this brief article, I will explain a few of its basics so that you can get a picture of what reality therapy is. In 1977, I learned the rudiments of *Control Theory* from William Powers, one of its early theorists. For many years, I called what I taught "control theory" even though from the beginning I deviated considerably from what Powers taught me. I did so because I wanted to use the theory in counseling, and much of what he taught me seemed impossible to adapt to this purpose.

Over the years, as I developed many new ideas and expanded the theory considerably, I became more and more dissatisfied with its name. It was the word "control" that bothered me. It was so hard for people to accept because it implies external control, which is repugnant to most people, and is the exact opposite of what is true. *It is, in fact, the theory of internal control.* So in April, 1996, I changed the name of what I teach to "choice theory." I did so because that name accurately describes the core of the theory, *we choose all we do*, and it is a concept that was an important part of reality therapy since it began in 1962. Also, it was not fair to Powers to continue to use that name when the theory I taught had so expanded and clarified his initial teachings that almost none of them remained. Therefore, if you read any of my many books, please change that name in your mind. It is only the name "control theory" that has been changed to "choice theory." Everything else remains the same.

Choice theory is a completely useful theory. Anyone who learns it can use it advantageously in his or her life; hence, a significant reality therapy technique is to teach clients choice theory. This way, when the therapy sessions come to an end, the client can continue the therapy on his or her own by applying choice theory to life as if the client were his or her own therapist, which, indeed, the client has become. Clients who are unable or unwilling to learn choice theory still can be helped, but they cannot avail themselves of this self-help component that is a significant addition to the therapy.

Choice theory explains that we all are motivated by pleasure which, in practice, means that whether or not we feel pain, we always want to learn how to behave to feel better. In the same sense, we all are motivated to avoid painful situations as soon as we recognize they may be painful. But choice theory also explains in detail that all pleasure and pain is derived from our efforts to satisfy *five basic needs* built into the our genes. These needs are the following: *survival, love and belonging, power, freedom,* and *fun*. All behavior that satisfies one or more of these needs is pleasurable. All behavior that attempts, but fails, to satisfy one or more of these needs is painful.

Choice theory also explains that *all we can do from birth to death is behave, that we choose all behavior that attempts to satisfy our needs, and that all behavior should be considered total behavior.* Total because it is always made up of four components: *acting, thinking, feeling,* and the *physiology* that accompanies our actions, thoughts, and feelings. But of these four components, only two, acting and thinking, are *voluntary*. The other two, feelings and physiology, are *involuntary*; they depend on how successful our actions and thoughts are in satisfying our needs.

Therefore, when we practice reality therapy, we do not focus on feelings or physiology because these components are not directly under our control. All we can do is change our actions and thoughts; that is where we focus. It is not that we do not allow clients to tell us how they feel or talk about their physiology, but we always go back to actions and thoughts by saying, *if you want to feel better, you must change how you are acting and thinking.*

While we do not choose our dreams, twitches, or tics, I believe we choose our delusions and hallucinations. How we do this is impossible to explain in this short article. It has been my experience, however, that, if you ask, clients almost always can tell you when they chose to stop hallucinating or deluding. And it is always because they learned to choose more need-satisfying total behaviors. When they did, the hallucinations and delusions were no longer necessary. Their life was now in effective control without hallucinations and delusions.

Choice theory explains that *the purpose of all behavior is to control our lives so that we feel better.* Just as we may find love and feel in control of our lives when we do, a psychotic person feels more control of his or her life when hallucinating. And a psychotic person feels more pleasure when he or she hallucinates than before he or she made this choice. Therefore, the *purpose of therapy is to help people make more responsible choices that give them more effective control over their lives and that feel better.* This does not mean feel better as soon as possible; it means learning that some things take a long time and a lot of planning but, in the end, the purpose is always to feel better. No one works hard in the hopes of feeling worse.

An example of an irresponsible choice is to choose to take addicting drugs. These drugs feel good, not because they help satisfy a need, but because they mimic the pleasure that is felt when a need is satisfied. In taking them, a person can choose to destroy his or her life while feeling good in the process. Thus, the reality therapy and choice theory definition of *responsible* is to satisfy your own needs while not depriving yourself or another person of the chance to satisfy his or her needs.

If we choose all our behavior for the purpose of satisfying our basic needs, then it follows that all of our behavior is internally motivated. This means that choice theory stands in direct opposition to the traditional psychological theory that almost all the world embraces—Stimulus-Response (S-R) Theory. S-R theory contends that we are externally motivated and that our behavior is a response to an external stimulus. If this were true, few clients could change; they would be at the mercy of the world instead of in control, or attempting to gain effective control, of their lives. We may not be in effective control when we seek counseling or are sent to counseling, but we are in control of what we are now choosing to do.

The purpose of reality therapy is to help clients make better choices—the kind of choices that lead them in the direction of taking effective control of their lives. When they are better able to do this, the active phase of counseling is over, but they can continue to use choice theory for the rest of their lives and may not need any more counseling.

In actual practice, we do not focus on the needs but on what we can do to gain and maintain pleasurable human relationships, because it is only through these relationships that we can satisfy our needs. For example, driven by the need to survive, we may be hungry and can not find food on our own. We look for someone to help us and feel good if he or she does. The same holds for warmth and shelter. Because we all have the need to love and belong, it is necessary to have a good relationship with another human being to satisfy this need. In order to feel powerful, at a minimum, someone must listen to what we have to say. For us to feel free, we must have the idea that others do not control us and that we have the freedom to choose what we do with our lives. And while it may be possible to have fun on your own, it is much easier with others. *Therefore, we are, by nature, social beings.*

When a client comes into the office and says he or she feels bad, at that moment I know that, no matter what has or has not happened in the past, this client is unable to gain the kind of human relationships he or she needs right now. Therefore, almost all those who come or are sent for counseling are lonely. The reality therapist recognizes this and makes a strong effort to create a good relationship with all clients. But choice theory also teaches what is wrong with all relationships—something that, at first glance, may seem unbelievably simple.

This is that all people who need counseling, or are having any difficulty living their lives, have essentially one, two, three, or four variations of the same problem. First, someone is trying to make the client do what he or she does not want to do. Second, the client is trying to make someone else do what that person does not want to do. Third, each is trying to make the other do what the other does not want to do. Fourth, it is also very common for us to attempt to make ourselves do something we do not want to do, and we are frustrated when this effort fails.

Think back into your own life and you will see that whenever you were unhappy, one or more of these common variations was the problem. Because you can pinpoint the problem quickly does not mean that this problem is easy to solve. It is usually difficult, for some people almost impossible, to solve. But, difficult or easy, the reality therapist knows this is the problem and, knowing this, he or she has a good chance to focus the counseling and get it started quickly. Because any problem with relationships is always in the present, reality therapy focuses on the present. By doing so, reality therapy is usually effective in a reasonable amount of time. Twelve sessions can go a long way in the hands of a skilled reality therapist.

Counseling is difficult because most clients do not want to focus on the present; they want to go back to the past and blame their unhappiness on someone else. Because the client has no control over any of these people and certainly has no way of changing what they did in the past, this way to counsel takes the counseling down a dead end. As long as the counselor is willing to stay in the past, nothing can be accomplished. The client may be satisfied and feel better because of the attention and because he or she has found someone who agrees, but the real problem will not be touched.

The real task of the reality therapist, using choice theory as his or her guide, is to keep all clients in the present and only go back into the past to see if there was an effective past behavior that can be of use now. But it is not enough to persuade clients to stay in the present. They must also learn that the only person who can change the present *whom they can control* is themselves. For example, it does no good for a woman or a man to say that he or she wants more attention from his or her spouse. All each can do is try to figure out how to give the other more attention, which might persuade the other to change. Each might have to do this even though there is no assurance that the other will give more attention in return. But, if neither will make the effort, as many will not, there is nothing that can be done. So the choice is between something and nothing, and reality therapy offers something. And, in the hands of a skilled therapist, this something is often highly effective.

To facilitate this process, teaching the client choice theory may be essential. When the client learns why he or she is doing what he or she is doing and learns that he or she can control only his or her own behavior, the client is, with the therapist's guidance, usually able to use this information well and therapy begins to move along. Without this theory, both counselor and client may flounder.

For example, when a client comes into the office, as stated previously, I know what the problem is. The client, right now, is having a relationship problem, and that problem is because someone else is not treating the client the way he or she wants to be treated. Or the client is trying to do something he or she really does not want to do (e.g., love someone he or she does not love). Using reality therapy based on choice theory, the counselor will start to focus on two things and continue this focus throughout therapy because these two things are all the client, or anyone, in or out of counseling, can change.

1.   What do you want right now?
2.   What are you choosing to do right now?

The counselor also will listen to the client relating how badly he or she feels. But knowing that none of us can change our feelings without changing what we do, the counselor should explain to the client that he or she can not change the way he or she feels unless he or she chooses a new behavior. As soon as possible, the counselor will teach the client that the only person's behavior he or she can control is his or her own, that the client is choosing all he or she does, that the client has no way of changing others, and that all that the client can give to another human being is information. We cannot change people; they alone can choose to change the way they act and think.

To do what is suggested above, the counselor must be able to create a strong positive relationship with all sorts of clients. Without this relationship, the client will not listen to the counselor, and nothing will happen. As the counselor is focusing on the real problem of the client, something the client is trying to avoid, creating this relationship may seem difficult in the beginning. But most clients, at some level, know that their problem is now, that it is with people, and that they only can change themselves. So if the counselor stands firm in this belief, it is my experience that clients change quickly. They really are looking for someone who will be firm enough to persuade them to abandon the irresponsible, evasive behaviors that have gotten them into the trouble they are in.

All that I have explained is difficult to do. It takes a lifetime of practice to do this well. I have been at it for 40 years, and I still am learning. Each counselor develops his or her own techniques, and no counselor will succeed unless he or she spends a lot of time analyzing and evaluating his or her therapy practices each day. Finally, if counselors do not apply the choice theory that they are learning to their own lives, they will not be able to practice reality therapy effectively.

In this brief article, I have not come close to explaining choice theory to the extent needed for gaining competence in reality therapy. To learn this, the following books must be studied, and some training with the William Glasser Institute is strongly advised. The address of the William Glasser Institute is 22024 Lassen Street, Suite 118, Chatsworth, CA 91311. Suggested readings are the following:

Glasser, N. (1980). *What are you doing?* New York: HarperCollins.
Glasser, N. (1989). *Control theory in the practice of reality therapy.* New York: HarperCollins.
Glasser, W. (1965). *Reality therapy.* New York: HarperCollins.
Glasser, W. (1984). *Control theory.* New York: HarperCollins.
Glasser, W. (1985). *Staying together.* New York: HarperCollins.

USING STORIES IN THERAPY
WITH CHILDREN AND FAMILIES

Therapist: Larry Golden, Ph.D.

Affiliation: Psychologist; Associate Professor, The University of Texas at San Antonio; private practice.

Major works:
> Capuzzi, D., & Golden, L. (Eds.). (1988). *Preventing adolescent suicide.* Muncie, IN: Accelerated Development.
> Golden, L., & Norwood, M. (Eds.). (1993). *Case studies in child counseling.* New York: Macmillan.
> Herlihy, B., & Golden, L. (1990). *Ethical standards casebook.* Alexandria, VA: American Counseling Association.
> Author of two other books.

Population for whom the technique is appropriate: Children, adolescents, and families.

Cautionary notes: If you enjoy listening to stories yourself, you really will have fun with this creative approach. Storytelling is a gentle and safe way to teach important lessons. But do not expect too much!

Storytelling has become my therapeutic hobby. It gets my creative juices flowing. Storytelling is a right brain process that bypasses logic and argumentation and stimulates the imagination.

Finding the Right Story

I invite children and families to tell their own stories about the problems with which they are struggling in their lives. Then I find a match, a story that will serve as a cautionary tale or, perhaps, yield insight or inspiration. My sources are (a) my personal experience, (b) the experiences of other clients, (c) television and movies, and (d) literature.

How to Tell Stories

I come up with a story when therapy gets stuck. I usually do not provide the "moral of the story." Instead, I use the Colombo approach, providing lots of disclaimers—"You know, I heard this story and it somehow reminded me of you. I'm probably way off base, but it won't take much of your time." Let clients draw their own conclusions. Also, keep your stories short or clients might nod off.

Case Examples

I have begged, borrowed, and stolen my stories although I do not think any of them are copyrighted, so I guess that means that the reader can "borrow" them from me. I have attached a "moral" at the end of each story solely to drive home my point; again, let your clients draw their own conclusions.

The Empty Nest. A story can be very, very short. In this example, my client is a parent who is frustrated by the "boomerang" phenomenon. Her 24-year-old daughter leaves home in a door-slamming storm and then moves back into the household a few days later. I told this mother about how parent eagles destroy their nests after chicks take wing.

The moral: This was an antidote to the guilt that was maintaining a daughter's dependent behavior.

Out of Auschwitz. I shared this biographical sketch of Victor Frankl with a gifted, depressed, and underachieving teen.

Victor Frankl, the founder of Logotherapy, received his M.D. from the University of Vienna in 1930 and his Ph.D. in psychology from the same institution in 1949. But he learned the most profound lessons while imprisoned at Auschwitz and Dachau where his entire family was murdered under Nazi rule. What were these lessons? Frankl learned that he had the power to choose his own attitude under *any* circumstances. He also discovered that there were people in the camps in even worse shape than himself and who needed his help.

The moral: If Frankl could bring meaning to his life in Auschwitz, I suspect that my young client could do the same at Madison High.

Bluebonnets. This is a story told to me by a client; I'll call her Elena. Elena and her three kids had been abandoned by her abusive husband. She had been diagnosed with lupus. Her children were acting up in school. She was bent down beneath serious problems.

She told me this true story. On the long return drive to San Antonio from Corpus Christi where she and her children had visited family, her ancient clunker developed a flat tire. The last straw! Elena and her kids climbed up a hill to look for signs of civilization. Nada! Zip! But then they saw a lake. On closer inspection, the apparent lake was a sea of bluebonnets shining in the sun. This vision transfixed the family. But eventually, reluctantly, Elena and her children hiked back to their car. A Good Samaritan had already stopped to help.

The moral: No profound insights here, just a lovely vision of how the world could be.

Mary's Path. I have told this true story to clients who are immobilized by guilt and tragedy.

Becky left her baby in the bathtub to answer the phone. There was only an inch or so of water in the tub. The baby managed to turn on the hot water, was scalded, and died.

Becky's friends tried to help: "You need to stop blaming yourself. You didn't mean any harm." Becky began drinking heavily.

Salvation came through a Catholic priest: "The only way out is confession and a life of penitence." Subsequently, Becky hooked up with Alcoholics Anonymous and enrolled in our counselor education program at The University of Texas at San Antonio. Now she is employed as a chemical dependency counselor with an indigent population.

The moral: There is no easy way, but there is a way.

The Rattlesnake. This is a cautionary tale that I have found helpful with adolescents who are not sufficiently respectful of addictive substances.

An old Texas cowboy was resting at the top of a high hill on a sunny day as a "Blue Norther" blew in. He knew he would have to get off the hilltop pronto or freeze. Just then he saw a rattler and, to his amazement, it spoke to him: "I came out to sun myself, but now I'm freezing to death. I don't have the energy to return to my warm burrow. Please help me."

"If I help you, how do I know you won't strike me?"

"Come now," said the snake, "Would I do that to someone who saved my life?"

So the cowboy carried the snake to the edge of its burrow. Quick as lightning, the snake bit him.

With his dying breath the cowboy asked, "How could you?"

"You knew I was a snake, and that's what snakes do."

The moral: Don't kid yourself. You *know* what drugs are capable of.

MEMORY WORK WITH CHILDREN

Therapist: Linda Goldman, M.S.

Affiliation: Certified Professional Counselor, Certified Grief Therapist; Certified Grief Educator; private grief therapy practice and consultant, Family Support Center, Kennsington, Maryland.

Major works:
> Goldman, L. (1994). *Life and loss: A guide to help grieving children.* Muncie, IN: Accelerated Development.
> Goldman, L. (1996). *Breaking the silence: A guide to help children with complicated grief.* Bristol, PA: Taylor & Francis.

Population for whom the technique is appropriate: I use memory work in my grief therapy with children. These are children who have suffered the loss of a loved one who has been very close to them. The children's ages range from 5 to 12, with some techniques continuing into adolescence. I work with children in 45- to 55-minute sessions in private grief therapy using photographs, treasured objects, drawing, writing in memory books, or tape recordings and videos.

Cautionary notes: None.

Memory Books

Memory books are participatory workbooks that enable children to draw and write their feelings and thoughts in an interactive way. They can be purchased commercially or made specifically to meet the needs of the child. The following are ideas I have used that have been helpful to children:

- Draw how you found out your loved one died.
- Draw the funeral.
- If you could see your loved one, one more time, what would you say? What would he or she say to you?
- If you could change one thing or do one thing over, what would it be? (This brings out any guilty feelings.)
- Draw what your family was like before your loved one died. Draw what your family is like now.
- What is your funniest memory of your loved one?

- Write a letter to your loved one. Tell him or her how you feel about his or her death. (Specify if the death is suicide or homicide.)
- List or draw what you worry about since your love one died.

Memory Boxes or Memory Tables

We can help children create a memory box or a memory table to provide places to store treasured items of their loved ones. Memory boxes can be made from a shoe box that is painted and decorated to house precious belongings. A special table can be displayed in the child's room with pictures and other objects that are meaningful to the child. This table also can be a part of the therapeutic environment. Children can begin by bringing in one picture or special object and sharing about it. They can bring in more *when they are ready.*

Photos, Videos, and Tape Recordings

Photographs, videos, and tape recordings are concrete ways to stimulate visual and auditory memories of a loved one. Making a photo album of pictures children choose and having it titled "My Life" brings in a clear picture of times and events shared as well as motivation for discussion. So often kids feel they might forget how their loved one looked and sounded. These are tangible ways to facilitate memory work.

CREATING VISION, MISSION, AND VALUES
FOR COUPLES IN COUNSELING

Therapist: Russell Grieger, Ph.D.

Affiliation: Licensed Clinical Psychologist; Russell Grieger and Associates, a leadership and organizational consulting company.

Major works:
> Ellis, A., & Grieger, R. (Eds.). (1977). *Handbook of rational-emotive therapy, Volume I.* New York: Springer.
> Ellis, A., & Grieger, R. (Eds.). (1986). *Handbook of rational-emotive therapy, Volume II.* New York: Springer.
> Grieger, R., & Boyd, J. (1980). *Rational-emotive therapy: A skills based approach.* New York: Van Nostrand Reinhold.

Population for whom the technique is appropriate: Any individuals in couple counseling.

Cautionary notes: None.

It is quite common for companies to create both a Mission Statement (a statement of their purpose for existence) and a set of Organizational Values (a description of interpersonal and business principles). Together these serve to guide organizational decisions as well as individual and collective behavior.

In my role as an organizational consultant, I work with many businesses and professional entities around such issues as reorganization, conflict resolution, customer service, and strategic decision making. Regardless of the issue, I find it invaluable to direct and ground the organization in their mission statement (MS) and Values (Vs) in order to define their problems, set their direction, and determine their future courses of action to bring about desired results. Whenever organizations do this, they inevitably find solutions to their problems and cement trust and good will on their team.

As a Rational Emotive Behavior Therapist, when working with couples, I pay special attention to eliminating the irrational beliefs each party may hold that cause the anxiety, depression, hurt, and especially the anger that cripples affection and the ability to resolve differences. In typical REBT fashion, I help them identify, dispute, and replace these irrational beliefs.

Additionally, I have found that assisting couples in writing their "Marital Mission Statement" and "Values" is a powerful tool in helping them choose to act in ways that mutually benefit each other and the relationship. The MS and Vs serve as a beacon for correct action much like a lighthouse guides ships to shore. When two people participate fully and genuinely in creating these and then responsibly, without anger, use them to direct how they act with each other, their relationship often soars.

Case Example

Take, for example, part of the Mission Statement and Values of John and Mary, the anonymous names of a couple with whom I currently am working. Since they drafted these, and committed to daily acting consistent with what they have written, they have found new depths of affection and commitment in their relationship.

Our Purpose. To add to the meaning in life by giving to and receiving from each other mutual support, companionship, acceptance, and intimacy.

Our Values. We commit to these values to guide our attitudes and behavior with each other.

Empathy. We pledge to create an atmosphere of safety and security for each other by being willing to listen and acknowledge the other's thoughts, feelings, and desires without criticism, defensiveness, or unsolicited advice.

Acknowledgment. We will go out of our way to notice, appreciate, and acknowledge the positive actions of each other. While recognizing that we each are imperfect, we will take care to catch the other doing good and reinforcing that, as opposed to catch the other doing bad and criticizing.

Summary

In closing, let me make a few observations. One, couples typically need help in creating their Mission Statement and Values, as well as assistance in learning to appreciate each other's value. Two, the MS and Vs can serve as a basis for determining loving, positive, rewarding things to do for each other, things designed to move the relationship in a positive direction. Three, the MS and the Vs provide a tool for defining a problem as well as problem solutions. In other words, marital problems by definition are behaviors contrary to the MS and the Vs. Problem solutions are behaviors contrary to the problem and are indeed consistent with the MS and Vs. Finally, behaviors that violate the MS and Vs, ones that often serve to disrupt the relationship, can easily elicit irrational beliefs, which require REBT to bring couples therapy full circle.

ASSERTION STRATEGIES

Therapist: Paul A. Hauck, Ph.D.

Affiliation: Clinical Psychologist, University of Utah; private practice.

Major works:

Hauck, P. A. (1994). *The three phases of love.* Louisville, KY: Westminister John Knox Press.

Hauck, P. A. (1994). *Overcoming the rating game: Beyond self-love, beyond self-esteem.* Louisville, KY: Westminister John Knox Press.

Author of 12 other books.

Population for whom the technique is appropriate: All ages and both sexes.

Cautionary notes: None.

In my over 40 years of experience as a clinical psychologist, I have been able to observe that the major problem my clients have are the difficult people with whom they live or work. Standing up to these individuals, refusing to be dominated by them, and knowing how to prevent being taken advantage of and in general being made miserable by others has been a very frequent issue that I have had to confront with my clients. To that end, I have given much thought to the whole issue of assertion and aggression and have come up with a grand scheme that enables the counselor to help these individuals simply, forthrightly, and expeditiously.

When people complain to me about the difficulties they are having with others, I generally am able to point out to them that they are not observing the three principles of human interaction. The three principles are as follows:

1. You get the behavior you tolerate.
2. Others will not change until you change first.
3. What should you change?—Your excessive toleration.

I make the point clear that they must do something to themselves rather than wait on others to do something about these annoying people in their lives. How should they go about asserting themselves to get these people to change, and what must they change?

My answer to my clients includes the three basic things that they are seeking (a) cooperation, (b) respect, and (c) love. To achieve these goals, the following rules must be observed.

Rule 1. If people do something good to you, you do something good to them (+ = +).

Rule 2. If people do something bad to you and they do not realize that they are behaving badly, reason with them but only on two separate occasions (− = + × 2).

Rule 3. If people are inconsiderate a third time, do something equally annoying to them, but it must be done without (a) anger, (b) guilt, (c) other pity, (d) fear of rejection, (e) fear of physical harm, and (f) fear of financial harm (− = −).

I caution clients not to talk about their difficulties after more than one or two warnings or explanations. That is the very means by which the problems are reinforced in the first place. But to make sure that it is not necessary to get tougher with these troublemakers, it is always advised to make certain that they do understand that what they are doing is something that bothers us; they may not have known it. But once we have let them know that we disapprove of their actions and we have done this perhaps once or twice, then there is no point in going into a third or a thirtieth explanation. Should Rule 3 not work, however, we have four options.

Option 1. Toleration without resentment. If we are able to achieve this, the problem is over and we simply are waiting to lump the thing gracefully.

Option 2. Protest. One also could call this: going on strike, or declaring a cold war. To accomplish this we have to go back to Rule 3 and make these troublemakers increasingly uncomfortable every time they do the same thing to us. It will get to a point where someone is not going to be able to tolerate the pressure any longer, as is usually common in a strike, and then the problem will change. Someone will give in.

Option 3. If a person does not give in to you and you are not willing to give in to him or her, you can go to the third option, which is to get a separation or divorce (i.e., a literal separation or divorce within problem marriages or a figurative separation within other problem relationships). If a divorce is distasteful or not allowed in one's religion, then one can get an emotional divorce by living as brother and sister in the same home, one can get a voluntary separation, or one can get a legal separation. And of course, if there are no religious restrictions against divorce, then divorce is an option.

Option 4. Toleration with resentment. I recommend that my clients use any of the first three options because they eventually can lead to relief. Option 4 always creates more suffering.

When do people have a right to protest? When they are less than Just Reasonably Content (JRC). If you do not stand up for your rights you will experience four, long-term consequences.

1. You will be unhappy.
2. You probably will become emotionally disturbed.
3. You gradually will fall out of love (i.e., if the problem relationship is with a spouse).
4. You will want to end the relationship.

If people will not change, decide to put up with the problem and tolerate it without resentment (Option 1) or use Option 3 and make them as uncomfortable as they make you and continue to do this until one of you gives up. Interestingly enough, when you get into this confrontational strategy, it is fairly easy to predict who is going to win. It happens to be the person who cares the least about the relationship.

DEREFLECTION FOR DEPRESSION

Therapist: Rosemary Henrion, MSN, M.Ed., RN

Affiliation: Mental Health Professional; Licensed Professional Registered Nurse; Department of Veterans Affairs, Pensacola, Florida; private practice, Pensacola, Florida.

Major work:
> Henrion, R. P., & Crumbaugh, J. C. (1997). *Rediscovering new meaning and purpose in life.* Abilene, TX: Viktor Frankl Institute of Logotherapy Press.

Population for whom the technique is appropriate: Adolescents and adults in therapy.

Cautionary notes: None.

Many clients feel that they are not resolving their problems as readily as they would like, and they seem to continue just to talk about them with no real satisfying solutions. "Dereflection" is a term coined by Dr. Viktor E. Frankl, M.D., Ph.D. He is the founder of logotherapy and presently is referred to as the "Father of the Third School of Viennese Psychotherapy." Dereflection may be defined as clients taking the focus off their problematic areas and refocusing on meaningful goals—that is, transcending the self from the victim role to that of survivor. Dereflection is also a technique utilized in assisting clients with searching for new meaning in traumatic experiences. This technique helps clients expand a conscious awareness level and rise above the feeling of being trapped and looking despairingly toward the future. Logotherapy is basically futuristic in nature, and as clients begin to see the total picture of what has occurred to them, they will focus more on their strengths and eliminate their weaknesses.

The general procedure for utilizing this technique appropriately is encouraging clients to ventilate their thoughts/feelings relating to the problematic areas causing the greatest difficulty. Catharsis is the first phase of any therapeutic approach. The therapist is actively listening and picking up cues of the client's positive behaviors and subsequently bringing these behaviors to the client's attention. As clients develop an increased in-depth awareness of their positive attributes, their self-esteem also will increase. Soon these individuals begin to view themselves as unique human beings pursuing individualized goals that become productive and fulfilling. Clients may develop a cause/mission that intensifies a deepening and more meaningful future. Simultaneously, they feel a sense of freedom and a greater control over their lives that never before has been experienced. When clients choose to develop a structured method for this procedure, they proceed through these steps with minimal difficulty. Consequently, enjoying higher levels of the quality of life falls in place, and this can be experienced for the remainder of the clients' lives.

This technique has been utilized frequently in the logotherapeutic process and is very successful with clients in this treatment modality. Clients accomplish their goals by resolving their conflicts and reaching for new heights as they experience the process of moving through this maze. This aspect of dereflection is very rewarding for clients, and they accept the challenge readily knowing that they are worthwhile individuals with untapped potential of becoming the best that they can be. The most significant part of this approach is that it is easily available for those individuals who choose to take risks to improve their quality of life. The whole approach is a new way of looking at old problems, and it is never too late to begin this challenge.

THE LAST FIVE MINUTES TECHNIQUE

Therapist: Joseph W. Hollis, Ed.D.

Affiliation: National Board Certified Counselor; Licensed Psychologist; counselor educator; Professor of Psychology-Counseling Emeritus, Ball State University, Muncie, Indiana; publisher of psychologically-based books.

Major works:

> Hollis, J. W., & Hollis, L. U. (1969). *Personalizing information processes: Educational, occupational, and personal-social.* New York: Macmillan.
>
> Hollis, J. W., & Donn, P. A. (1979). *Psychological report writing: Theory and practice* (2nd ed.). Muncie, IN: Accelerated Development.
>
> Hollis, J. (1997). *Counselor preparation: Programs, faculty, trends* (9th ed.). Bristol, PA: Accelerated Development, a member of the Taylor & Francis Group. Greensboro, NC: National Board for Certified Counselors.

Population for whom the technique is appropriate: All clients—individual or group setting

Cautionary notes: None.

The last five minutes of a counseling/therapeutic session can serve for the client as a transition time between the counselor's office and the client's everyday environment. The counselor can help assure the client's productive reentry into his or her everyday environment by using the last five minutes to address confidentiality and disclosure—client disclosure, counselor disclosure, or both.

A counseling/therapeutic session generally includes the client discussing items that he or she wants kept in confidence—items that the client does not want family, friends, and associates from his or her everyday environment to know. Counselors honor the confidentiality of disclosures that occur during counseling sessions with the exception of those things that counselors must relate to authorities (e.g., physical or sexual abuse).

Actually, the possibility of revealing confidential material to another person is much more apt to be done by the client than by the counselor. The reason is that the client often becomes emotionally involved during the counseling session, and his or her defenses are lowered. Then, when the client leaves the counseling session and meets a friend who says, "What did you talk about today?" the client may tell the friend what was said, thereby making the information—intended to be confidential—available to another person.

Another point for counselors to consider is the client's concern about what the counselor may say about the counseling session to a certain other person or persons. For example, when a client is referred to a counselor and the client has revealed confidential information to the counselor, then the client may begin to wonder what the counselor will say to the referring person.

I use the final few minutes of each session not only to have the client identify the significant points covered during the session, but also to review the items that we discussed that could be passed on by the client to a friend, parent, teacher, or others. I often need to assist the client to enable him or her to be able to share some things with others without relating the confidential items.

Also, if another person is apt to ask me about the session, I ask the client to identify what I may or may not say to the person. This places the client and me on like terms and teaches the client how to be truthful without revealing confidential information. The items that the client wishes to keep confidential can be, and the client and I agree upon what is confidential and what, if we need to, can be shared with others.

When I was a school counselor, teachers often referred students to me. Students sometimes were concerned about what I might say to the referring teacher or to others. The student (client) desired to know, and I needed to be clear on what the student was willing for the teacher to know. The same kind of situation often occurs when counseling a young person and the parent asks, "What did my child discuss with you?"

Yes, the last five minutes may be some of the most important minutes of the session. We crystalize what we have done, and we identify what and how, if necessary, information should be shared outside the office. In addition, what we share in those last five minutes often becomes a source of reference points for future sessions.

COMMUNITY GENOGRAM: IDENTIFYING STRENGTHS

Therapist: Allen E. lvey, Ed.D., A.B.P.P.

Affiliation: Psychologist, Distinguished University Professor, University of Massachusetts, Amherst.

Major works:
> Ivey, A. (1971). *Microcounseling: Innovations in interviewing training, counseling psychotherapy and psychoeducation.* Springfield, IL: Thomas
>
> Ivey, A. (1986). *Developmental therapy: Theory into practice.* San Francisco: Jossey-Bass.
>
> Ivey, A., Ivey, M., & Simek-Morgan, L. (1997). *Counseling and psychotherapy: A multicultural perspective* (4th ed.). Boston: Allyn & Bacon.
> Author of over 20 other books and 200 articles or chapters.

Population for whom the technique is appropriate: Is appropriate for adults and adolescents, has been adapted for use with children successfully, and is useful in family therapy. Many people from nontraditional families find this approach more helpful than a family genogram as it allows a more contextual, culturally-sensitive approach.

Cautionary notes: See final two paragraphs of this technique.

This exercise has three goals: (a) to generate a narrative of story of the client in community context; (b) to help the client generate an understanding of how we all develop in relation to others; and (c) to use visual, auditory, or kinesthetic images as sources of strength. These images of strengths can be called upon later in the counseling and therapy interview as positive resources to help clients cope with life's difficulties.

In addition, this exercise will help you understand the cultural background of your client, for it is through family and community that we learn the cultural framework. Finally, many of your clients will have had difficult life experiences within their communities. They may be tempted to focus first on the negative as they develop their awareness and stories of how they developed and live in a community setting. While you will need to attend to potential negative stories, we urge you to focus on positive strengths.

Develop a Visual Representation of the Community

1. Consider a large piece of paper as representing your broad culture and community. It is recommended that you select the community in which you primarily were raised, but any other community, past or present, may be used.
2. Place yourself or the client in that community, either at the center or other appropriate place. Represent yourself or the client by a circle, a star, or other significant symbol.
3. Place your own or the client's family or families on the paper, again represented by the symbol that is most relevant for you. The family can be nuclear or extended or both.
4. Place important and most influential groups on the community genogram, again representing them by circles or other visual symbols. School, family, neighborhood, and spiritual groups are selected most often. For teens, the peer group is often particularly important. For adults, work groups and other special groups tend to become more central.
5. Connect the groups to the focus individual, perhaps drawing more heavy lines to indicate the most influential groups.

Search for Images and Narratives of Strengths

While you undoubtedly recognize that many individual difficulties and problems arise in a family, community, and cultural context, the community genogram focuses on strengths.

The community genogram provides a frame of reference to help the client see self-in-context. The client is asked to generate narratives of key stories from the community where he or she grew up. If relevant, key stories from the present living community also may be important. The emphasis is on positive stories from the community and positive images. The community genogram is kept and posted on newsprint during the entire counseling series of interviews.

The community genogram in its first stages focuses on positive stories and images. The importance of this point cannot be overstated. You will find that once this positive approach has been used first, clients have a foundation for exploring more difficult and troublesome areas of their lives. In addition, you will have a good foundation yourself as a therapist that helps you understand the community, family, and cultural background of the client.

The specifics of the positive search are as follows:

1. Focus on one single community group or the family. You or the client may want to start with a negative story or image. Please do not work with the negative until positive strengths are solidly in mind.

2. Develop a visual, auditory, or kinesthetic image that represents an important positive experience. Allow the image to build in your mind, and note the positive feelings that occur with the image. If you allow yourself or the client to fully experience that positive image, you may experience tears and/or strong bodily feelings. These anchored body experiences represent positive strengths that can be drawn upon to help you and your clients deal with difficult issues in therapy and in life.

3. Tell the story of the image. If it is your story, you may want to write it down in journal form. If you are drawing out the story from a client, listen sensitively.

4. Develop at least two more positive images from different groups within the community. It is useful to have one positive family image, one positive spiritual image, and one positive cultural image. Again, many of us will want to focus on negative issues. Hold to the search for positive resources.

5. Summarize the positive images in your own words and reflect on them. Encourage a client to summarize his or her learning, thoughts, and feelings in his or her own words. As you or your client thinks back, what occurs? Record the responses so that they may be drawn upon in many settings in therapy or in the daily life of the client.

The community genogram can be a very emotional and dramatic strategy. At a minimum, it will help you understand the special cultural background of your client, and it serves as a reservoir of positive experiences that can be drawn upon to help you and the client throughout therapy.

Cautions

Some clients will have difficulties in finding positive experiences. Work hard to find positive strengths and assets first. Tears often appear during imagery work. At times, severe issues within the community may need to be worked through before this more positive approach can be used. Children like to draw, and presenting their communities requires the usual creativity required when working with children.

I recommend posting the community genogram/chart (and often a family genogram/chart as well) throughout all counseling and therapy sessions. This helps the client remain aware of contextual issues and the fact that, as Jean Baker Miller stated, we are all a "self-in-relation."

Source: Copyright © 1995 by Allen E. Ivey, Box 226, Sunapee, NH 03782. Reprinted here by permission.

RELATIONSHIP-CENTERED COUNSELING: AN INTEGRATIVE HUMANISTIC APPROACH FOR DIVERSE PROBLEMS

Therapist: Eugene W. Kelly, Jr., Ph.D.

Affiliation: Licensed Professional Counselor; psychologist; Professor of Counseling, George Washington University, Washington, DC.

Major works:
> Kelly, E. W., Jr. (1977). *Effective interpersonal communication: A manual for skill development.* Washington, DC: University Press of America.
> Kelly, E. W., Jr. (1994). *Relationship-centered counseling: An integration of art and science.* New York: Springer.
> Kelly, E. W., Jr. (1995). *Spirituality and religion in counseling and psychotherapy diversity in theory and practice.* Alexandria, VA: American Counseling Association.

Population for whom the technique is appropriate: Adaptable to diverse populations.

Cautionary notes: None.

Introduction

I will use the term "approach" rather than "technique" to describe the application of relationship-centered therapy. My reason for this usage is that techniques or technical expertise, although inherent to the operation of relationship-centered therapy, are but one component of the total approach. More specifically, in relationship-centered therapy the relationship component is the primary, core component of all therapeutic applications, with technical expertise acting as the instrumental extension of the therapeutic relationship. I have given elsewhere a full exposition of the principles and research supporting and informing relationship-centered therapy (Kelly, 1994, 1995, 1996).

Relationship-centered therapy involves first a fundamental way of thinking about human development, counseling, and psychotherapy in terms of relationship. Relationship as used here means that (a) the relationship is the primary ground and context for development of the individual person and individual, in-depth subjectivity; (b) the therapeutic relationship is the primary, integrative core of counseling; and (c) and counseling process and outcome necessarily involve contributions of both client and counselor in relationship. Relationship-*centered* means that the therapeutic relationship is necessarily extended in therapeutic tasks and techniques appropriate to the needs of the client.

Application

Two major, practical consequences of the relationship-centered perspective are: (a) all relationship-facilitative conditions involve substantive participation and contributions by both the client and counselor, and (b) facilitative conditions extend into tasks and techniques that concretize the humanizing effect of the therapeutic relationship according to the specific needs of each client.

A brief case example will illustrate the concrete application of these two practical principles. The case involved a middle-age, college-educated female who was having persistent, debilitating anxious feelings stemming from what she regarded as a serious mistake in her work. The first part of my relationship-centered work with her consisted primarily of facilitative responses (e.g., empathic reflections and open-ended questions) that helped her expand upon and explore circumstances, feelings, and thoughts related to her mistake. A key relationship-centered variation on this basic client-centered approach was that my empathic responsiveness embraced not only the client's perspective understood individually but also the *relational* perspective that the two of us were developing gradually in our mutual responsiveness. Thus, my facilitative responses gradually came to include therapeutically relevant ideas and feelings as these were stimulated by the growing relational world that the client and I were coming to share. This concrete application of the relationship perspective (rather than an individualistic client self-perspective) means the following: rather than working simply from the client's self-center or viewing the counselor's initiatives as intrusions from outside the client's individuality, the *full* human resources of both the client and counselor are available for the client's unique personal development. Thus, the fully humanistic orientation of the relationship-centered approach is preserved.

The second major part of my work in this case was to extend with specific therapeutic actions the power of the therapeutic relationship and the insights gained in the facilitative-exploratory phase. I did this with several cognitive techniques. I used a guided discovery method in which I had Stephanie describe in detail how she handled all of the work elements connected with the one mistake that she made. By going over all the important actions associated with her work mistake, we were able to isolate her mistake from her other, competent behavior. We then questioned the importance of this one error and her self-attribution of incompetence. She then could see this one action in the perspective of her overall competent performance. With this she was able to shift from a self-devaluing concentration to a more relaxed acceptance of her mistake and to shift from a negative generalization based on a single error to a positive generalization based on her more typical pattern of behavior.

Conclusion

Relationship-centered therapy conceptually and practically bridges the divide between humanistic and technical approaches to counseling and psychotherapy. The integrity of the individual person is maintained by recognizing that personal development occurs in relationship (including therapeutic relationship). And the in-depth humanism of the relationship is legitimately expanded into technique by recognizing that technical expertise is an enhancement of our fundamental humanity.

References

Kelly, E. W., Jr. (1994). *Relationship-centered counseling: An integration of art and science.* New York: Springer.

Kelly, E. W., Jr. (1995, August). *Relationship-centered counseling: The integrative interaction of relationship and technique.* Paper presented at the 1995 national convention of the American Psychological Association, New York.

Kelly, E. W., Jr. (1996, April). *From client-centered to relationship-centered counseling: A humanistic integration.* Paper presented at the 1996 world conference of the American Counseling Association, Pittsburgh, PA.

CREATIVE COLLECTION OF THERAPEUTIC ADVENTURES: FEELINGS, FEARS, AND WORRIES

Therapist: Melissa T. Korenblat-Hanin, M.S.W.

Affiliation: Licensed Clinical Social Worker, The Asthma Center at Barnes-Jewish West County Hospital, St. Louis, Missouri.

Major works:

Korenblat-Hanin, M., & Moffet, M. (1993). *The asthma adventure book.* Rochester, NY: Fisons.

Author of *The Asthma Adventure Game* and *The Art of Relaxation* cassette tape.

Population for whom the technique is appropriate: Appropriate for children ages 5 to 12, in individual, group, or family therapy, designed for those coping with a chronic disease or who are dealing with personal or family change.

Cautionary notes: None.

Helping children express, explore, and understand their feelings can be a challenging and enjoyable process. It is my experience that creative communication allows children to identify, clarify, and express their feelings in pleasurable and non-threatening ways. Drawing, playing, and acting are familiar to all children and are just as poignant as verbalizations. The following creative play therapy activities are samples of how a therapist, counselor, or facilitator might focus on various feelings. These activities are a blueprint for working with children who are coping with chronic illnesses such as asthma, diabetes, or cancer as well as children who are dealing with personal or family changes (e.g., birth of a baby, divorce, separation, parental remarriage, new step family, or death).

Hide-and-Go-Seek Feelings (Ages 5 to 8)

Activity Objective. This activity allows the younger child to search, find, and identify various feelings. It also illustrates the importance of getting feelings out and the effects on the physical body if feelings are kept inside.

Materials Needed. Construction paper, scissors, markers, tape, and candy.

Instructions.

1. Prior to the session, the facilitator prepares a set of four feeling faces on construction paper. The feelings include happy, mad, sad, and scared. There should be one set of feelings per child.
2. The faces should be cut out in the shape of a circle. Candy is taped to the back of each circle. These feeling faces are hidden around the room.
3. The facilitator begins the session by discussing the importance of feelings and how they can affect our body if they are kept inside (e.g., stomachaches or headaches).
4. The activity begins with the facilitator telling the children that there are feelings hidden around the room and their task is to find the feelings.
5. Upon completion of their search, they are instructed to share their feelings by making sure that each child has a complete set of the four feelings.
6. Once each child has one happy, one sad, one mad, and one scared feeling face, the children are asked the following about each feeling:
   • Pick one of the feeling faces and demonstrate what that feeling looks like.
   • What about your chronic disease or family changes makes you feel that particular feeling?
   • Where does that feeling get stuck in your body? (That feeling face then is taped on the spot on their body that is specified, demonstrating that they were able to get their feelings out.)
7. The children may eat the candy from the back of the feeling faces (symbolizing ownership of that feeling).
8. Each child should be validated while he or she is expressing feelings as well as while he or she is wearing the feelings on the outside of his or her body.
9. The children then participate in a feeling march, walking around the room wearing their feelings on the outside. (Alternative option: The feeling march can be videotaped so that the group may refer to it later and parents can be invited in to watch the feeling march.)

Feeling Collage (Ages 6 to 12)

Activity Objective. This activity allows the children to express the numerous feelings they have (about, for example, their families' divorce or changes or chronic disease) in a collage format.

Materials Needed. Large drawing paper or poster board, scissors, magazines, pens, and glue.

Instructions.

1. The group members are given magazines, large drawing paper or poster board, scissors, and glue.
2. The group members are instructed to cut out pictures that describe how they feel about their chronic disease or family change.
3. The pictures are glued onto their poster board in order to create a collage.
4. The group members then write descriptive sentences to narrate the pictures. The final collage is shared with the group and discussed.

Feeling Movements (Ages 5 to 7)

Activity Objective. This movement exercise helps children identify various feelings and think about how the feelings would be expressed by using body movements.

Instructions.

1. The facilitator asks the group members to stand on one side of the room.
2. When various feeling states are called out by the facilitator (or group member), the group members will take three steps that express that feeling by using their body language. For example: mad steps might be taken in a stomping manner, and happy steps might be taken in hops.
3. The facilitator also can announce creative steps such as

   - 5 mad elephant steps
   - 3 sad turtle steps
   - 2 happy kangaroo steps
   - 1 scared rabbit step

The Feeling Forest (Ages 8 to 12)

Activity Objective. This activity helps convey the message that there are numerous feelings that people may have, and all feelings are equally important.

Materials needed. Paper, markers, pens, and pencils.

Instructions.

1. The facilitator may begin by describing a forest where artists carved faces in all the trees and now the trees have feelings and are able to express themselves.
2. The participants then will draw their perceptions of a feeling forest. This would include various feelings they are experiencing (in relation to their disease or family or personal changes). The trunks of the trees could include written explanations describing why they have the feeling, and the tops of the trees could include the feeling. Group members then share about their forest. The pictures may be displayed together to create a greater forest effect.

Anger Oath (Ages 5 to 8)

Activity Objective. After identifying sources for their anger, group members create and practice safe and acceptable ways to let their anger out.

Materials Needed. Pen, paper, and pillow (optional).

Instructions.

1. Each group member creates a top 10 angry list of the things that make them the angriest (focus on family changes, divorce, asthma, diabetes, etc.).
2. The group creates a list of safe ways to express angry feelings (e.g., stomping feet, running outside, punching a pillow, yelling into a pillow, riding a bike, telling someone, tearing up paper, or coloring).
3. The facilitator announces each idea, and group members simulate each idea by acting it out or, when feasible, actually doing the specific activity.
4. Group members raise their right hand and repeat after the facilitator "The Anger Oath": *I promise to remember that all my feelings are O.K., especially mad feelings. I promise to remember to get my mad feelings out in a safe say so that they do not hurt anybody, anything, or myself. I promise!*
5. The oath also could be in the form of a written contract that each group member signs and takes home.

Worry Dolls (Ages 5 to 10)

Activity Objective. This activity focuses on assisting children with their worries and encouraging them to share their worries. It allows children to learn how to feel comfortable verbalizing their worries and to learn that sharing their worries tends to make the worries seem less fearsome.

Materials Needed. Pipe cleaners, yarn, scissors, paper, and pen.

Instructions.

1. Discuss the purpose and importance of getting worries out and sharing them with others.
2. Have the children create worry dolls from pipe cleaners and yarn. (Alternative option: The children also could bring in their favorite stuffed animal.)
3. For younger children, the worry dolls should be created prior to the group meeting.
4. Each group member should participate in naming his or her worry doll and then telling the doll two or his or her worries.
5. The group also could create a worry list that would include all of their worries. This list could be revisited during future sessions, and when the children move on from their worries, they can be checked off the list.
6. Inform the children that each night before they go to sleep, they can use their worry doll by giving one of their worries to the doll.

Bugaboo (Ages 6 to 10)

Activity Objective. The group members express, through art media, their feelings about family changes or their chronic disease (and the medications they require).

Materials needed. Markers, construction paper, and pens. (Optional materials include string, stapler, tape, or glue.)

Instructions.

1. The facilitator explains how this activity will assist the children with their feelings about their medication, disease, or family changes.
2. The children are instructed to create a bug (younger children might need a pre-drawn bug) and draw or write inside the bug what "bugs them" about their medicines, disease, or family changes. A discussion should follow.
3. Each bug can be displayed individually or the group may create a group

"bugaboo book," a bug collage, or a bug chain (linking all the pictures together).

Fish, Wishes, Worries, and Fears (Ages 5 to 11)

Activity Objective. This active experience allows participants to "go fishing" while identifying the wishes and worries that they have about their disease or family changes.

Materials Needed: Poster board, scissors, markers/crayons, string, sticks, straws, adhesive magnets, tape, and Velcro.

Instructions.

1. Participants cut out three fish shapes from poster board and write on the fish three fears, wishes, or worries that they are experiencing.
2. Participants, with the facilitator's help, attach magnets, double stick tape, or Velcro to the fish so they can be caught. Poles are made from straws, sticks, construction paper, or string and a corresponding connecting device. If participants are young or time is limited, the above can be prepared by the facilitator.
3. Participants then try to catch a fish using the poles.
4. As they reel in their fear, worry, or wish, they discuss how they can let it go or why they need to keep it.
5. If a fish is caught that describes a fear the child does not have or a wish that is unrealistic, it is thrown back.
6. The fears or wishes collected can be attached to paper where they are discussed at future sessions. When a child has moved on from a particular fear, wish, or worry, he or she can cast it back.

Fly Your Fears Away (Ages 5 to 10)

Activity Objective. Group members will create paper airplanes to fly that illustrate the message that fears do not seem so burdensome and frightening once they are identified, shared, and out in the open.

Materials Needed. Paper and pens.

Instructions.

1. The facilitator will instruct the participants on the construction of paper airplanes.

2. On the inside of the airplanes, the participants will write or draw their fears about their asthma, diabetes, divorce, etc.
3. The airplanes are flown and targeted towards a wall or in a direction where nothing will be harmed and other group members are kept safe.
4. This is followed by a group discussion about the significance of sharing one's fears in order to reduce them. This discussion also echoes the importance of the idea that once fears are expressed, they tend to seem less frightening.

Musical Feelings (Ages 5 to 12)

Activity Objective. The children will translate their feelings and perceptions about their chronic disease or family changes into musical sounds. Music will be an alternate avenue for children to explore and express their feelings.

Materials Needed. Musical instruments.

Instructions.

1. The group members select instruments that when played will reflect their feelings.
2. The children are requested to create sounds that reflect their feelings about their disease or family changes, being attentive to intensity, pitch, duration, and frequency.
3. This activity can be recorded so that each child could take home a cassette of the sounds of the feelings.
4. This activity also could take the shape of a musical charade, whereby the group members who are listening also could have the opportunity to guess what feeling or feelings are being played.
5. After completion of their musical feeling ensemble, the children would explain their creation.

Summary

Feelings may seem foreign to children and families because many times they are kept hidden and secret. It also may not be safe to share one's feelings, because family members may not know how to begin to express themselves. Creative play therapy provides alternate avenues for communicating one's thoughts and feelings in a safe and enjoyable way. This treatment modality allows children to have fun while helping them crystallize feelings that used to be confusing and hidden. This exploration is an ongoing process that strengthens and builds the skills necessary to enhance healthy communication of feelings within the young child, adolescent, and family.

THE SET COMMUNICATION SYSTEM STRATEGY

Therapist: Jerold J. Kreisman, M.D., F.A.P.A.

Affiliation: Board Certified Psychiatrist; Associate Clinical Professor, St. Louis University School of Medicine, Department of Psychiatry; Director of Adult Psychiatric Services, St. Vincent's Psychiatric Division, DePaul Health Center, St. Louis, Missouri.

Major work:
> Kreisman, Jerold, J. (1991). *I hate you don't leave me: Understanding the borderline personality.* New York: Avon.

Population for whom the technique is appropriate: This strategy is highly recommended for clients diagnosed with borderline personality disorder who are in crisis. Although SET was developed specifically to help borderlines, it is often useful for other clients who respond to concise, consistent communication, even though they may not be in crisis.

Cautionary notes: None.

SET, which stands for *support, empathy, and truth,* is a unique three-part system of communication. SET is a valuable technique the therapist can utilize when confronting a borderline client or helping him or her make a decision or work through a crisis.

The "S" in SET is the "support" stage characterized by a personal statement of concern. "I am sincerely concerned about your current feelings and situation," is an example of a support statement. The therapist conveys his or her own feelings with a message that he or she will attempt to help.

The "E" or "empathy" stage is intended to acknowledge the borderline's chaotic feelings: "You seem to be saying that you feel absolutely dreadful today." It is imperative that the helper use empathy rather than sympathy ("I just feel so badly for you.") inasmuch as borderlines often will respond to sympathy with anger and rage, feeling that the therapist is being merely condescending. The empathy should focus on the client rather than on the therapist's feelings. Hence, a therapist who said, "I know exactly how terrible you are feeling" often would be criticized by the borderline patient who would exclaim that the therapist does not truly understand the client's reaction. When this occurs, conflict is evident.

The "T" in the SET model represents "truth" or reality. The "T" segment emphasizes that the client is ultimately responsible for his or her own life. Unlike support and empathy statements that are necessarily subjective, truth statements focus on the practical issue of what can be enacted to solve the problem. The therapist in this stage might say, "All right, now what can you do about it?" The therapist keeps his or her verbalizations very matter of fact. ("Okay, here's the situation. . . . Here is what is going to transpire if you don't change. . . . This is how I can be of service to you. . . . What steps will you take to handle this situation?") It is important to note that the therapist should avoid blame or sadistic punishment statements. ("This situation is a disaster for both of us! You knew the consequences, now live with them!") The truth portion of the SET paradigm is the most difficult for the borderline personality who routinely ignores or distorts realistic consequences.

Communication with the borderline ideally should include all three of the aforementioned messages (i.e., SET). Often communication with the borderline suffers because the message from the therapist is not clear or is not "heard."

If, for example, this occurred in the initial or so-called support stage, the borderline would perceive and accuse the therapist of not caring. Statements such as "You don't want to be involved," or "You couldn't care less about me," typically indicate that support statements were not integrated into the psychotherapeutic process.

When the empathy part of the message is not communicated well, the borderline will protest that he or she is misunderstood. ("You really have no idea how I'm feeling.") The borderline will not value a therapist who cannot appreciate his or her distress.

When the truth component is not clearly expressed or perceived, a precarious situation often manifests itself. Simply put, the borderline will wrongly assume that his or her perceptions are shared by others and that others truly are responsible for his or her ills. Worse yet, the borderline will have unrealistic expectations. Eventually, however, frustration will set in and the client-therapist relationship can collapse with the borderline harboring intense anger and disappointment.

TIME TRIPPING

Therapist: Arnold A. Lazarus, Ph.D.

Affiliation: Clinical Psychologist, Graduate School of Applied & Professional Psychology, Rutgers University, New Brunswick, New Jersey.

Major works:
> Lazarus, A. A. (1971). *Behavior therapy and beyond.* New York: McGraw Hill.
> Lazarus, A. A. (1976). *Multimodal behavior therapy.* New York: Springer.
> Lazarus, A. A. (1989). *The practice of multimodal therapy.* Baltimore, MD: Johns Hopkins University Press.
> Author of 13 other books and father of multimodal therapy.

Cautionary notes: None.

A method I called "Time Projection with Positive Reinforcement" (Lazarus, 1968) has proved successful with a number of people who became depressed after an annoying or distressing incident. Often, an event that caused intense aggravation or sorrow can be viewed with indifference or detachment after, say, a lapse of six months or a year. This is probably because the passage of time permits new or competing responses to emerge (and that is why "time heals"). So what would happen if, in a single session, a patient vividly imagined going forward in time, day by day, week by week, while clearly visualizing enjoyable activities in which he or she could engage? And then, when looking back at the distressing event from the vantage point of at least six months imagined time lapse, would the individual experience a diminution of negative affect? An affirmative answer has been obtained from a variety of people who were capable of actively immersing themselves in a sequence of positive imaginal events.

One of the first cases I reported was a 23-year-old woman who became acutely depressed when her boyfriend rejected her. A single time-projection session made a profound difference. She was asked to picture herself engaging in activities that she found rewarding—horseback riding, playing the guitar, painting, sculpting, attending concerts, and being in the country. In the session, she was asked to dwell on each pleasant event one by one, to imagine herself actually enjoying them. Soon the days would start flying past; they would turn into weeks and then into months. She was asked to recount how many rewarding activities had been sampled. We dwelled on these pleasing events for a while, and then I said, "Now pretend that six real months have gone by. How do you feel when you now reflect back to the incident that bothered you? It's now more than six months old."

She stated: "How can I put it in words? Let me just explain it in three ways. First, I feel kind of foolish; second, there are lots of pebbles on the beach; and number three, there's something inside that really wants to find an outlet on canvas. Does that make sense?"

A week later, the client reported that her appetite had returned, she was sleeping well again, and she had enjoyed many productive hours. Thereafter, she continued making satisfactory progress.

Future time-projection using images of positive reinforcement is no cure for deep-seated depression. But it has shown itself to be a rapid and lasting means for helping people with minor depressions who otherwise could very well have remained needlessly unhappy and distressed for considerable periods of time. Scores of people who suffered minor depressions over specific events have been helped by this time projection technique.

There are also many instances when it is expedient to travel back in time. For example, many clients carry grudges or otherwise remain affected by past hurts and indignities. When these individuals remain unresponsive to the usual therapeutic procedures—cognitive disputation and reframing, discussion and ventilation, formal desensitization, and so forth—time tripping into the past is often effective (again, only with people who are responsive to imagery procedures).

Thus, a 25-year-old man was extremely distressed about an event that occurred on his eighth birthday. Time tripping was employed as follows: "Try to imagine that we have a time machine and that you can travel back in time. You enter the time machine, and within a few moments you have gone back to that incident when you were unfairly punished in front of strangers. As you step out of the time machine, you are your present age, and you see your alter ego, yourself at age eight. Can you imagine that?"

The client answered affirmatively and the time tripping continued: "The eight-year-old senses something special about this adult man who has just entered the picture. He doesn't realize, of course, that you are the same little boy, all grown up, out of the future. Nonetheless, he will pay close attention to you. You can really get through to him."

The time tripping procedure then had the client reassuring his alter ego and providing succor, support, understanding, and an explanation of the intentions behind the perpetrator's (his father's) misguided actions. The client then was asked to step back into the time machine and return to the present so that we could analyze and review the impact of his excursion. This method often yields a rapid cognitive reframing of and desensitization to unpleasant memories.

I have described one seemingly intractable case, a 32-year-old woman who conjured up image after image, retrieved "forgotten memories," instituted a series of "court scenes" against her offenders, and introduced several other novel ways of coming to terms with past agonies. This process extended over seven months of weekly sessions before she finally declared, "I have worked all that out of my system" (Lazarus, 1989). In most instances, time tripping, either into the future or back to the past, is a rapid means of dispelling various forms of emotional distress.

References

Lazarus, A. A. (1968). Learning theory and the treatment of depressions. *Behaviour Research and Therapy, 6,* 83-89.

Lazarus, A. A. (1989). The practice of rational-emotive therapy. In M. E. Bernard & R. DiGiuseppe (Eds.), *Inside rational-emotive therapy.* New York: Academic Press.

THE FOUR-STEP EXPERIENTIAL SESSION
FOR DEEP-SEATED PERSONALITY CHANGE

Therapist: Alvin R. Mahrer, Ph.D.

Affiliation: Clinical psychologist; University of Ottawa, Canada; private practice.

Major works:
> Mahrer, A. R. (1989). *Dream work in psychotherapy and self-change.* New York: Norton.
> Mahrer, A. R. (1996). *The complete guide to experiential psychotherapy.* New York: Wiley.
> Author of 11 books and over 200 publications.

Population for whom the technique is appropriate: An experiential session is appropriate for virtually any adult, in virtually any state or condition, with virtually any painful scene of bad feeling.

Cautionary notes: None.

Think in terms of just one experiential session. Although the client is free to have as many sessions as he or she wishes, each session is its own complete mini-therapy, is open-ended, and usually takes one to two hours.

One aim is for the person to be a qualitatively new person. The person can get a taste, a sample, of what it can be like to be the optimal kind of person he or she is capable of being. Whether it is for just a few minutes or for much longer, the shift into being a whole new person is dramatic, radical, and qualitative.

The other aim is for the new person to be free of the situation of bad feelings. Whatever this person identifies as the scene of bad feelings, the aim is for the new person to be free of that scene of bad feeling. It is no longer a part of this person's world, and the bad feeling is essentially gone.

Strategy

In the session, the strategy is to go through four steps:

Step 1. Start from a scene of strong feeling, then find a powerful scene of powerful feeling, and then probe inside to discover the hidden, deeper way of being and experiencing. The session starts by going directly to the kind of feeling that the person is concerned about, worried, and pained by, and the scene or situational context in which this feeling occurs. "What is it that bothers you most, that is the worst thing for you, the feeling that is most painful? What is the situation, the time and place, when this feeling is strong?" He feels so alone and lonely on Sunday afternoons when he is all alone and almost crying. She feels worst when she and her boyfriend have those awful fights, and he says such terrible things about her.

Go from these scenes of strong feeling to even more powerful scenes in which these feelings were even more powerful. His bad feeling was powerful when he is a boy, and his father tells him that his mother had been killed in a car accident. She remembered the painful feeling as most intense when she had been beaten up by the drunken guy from the next apartment, and she is knocked to the floor by his blows.

When the patient is living and being in the powerful scene of powerful feeling, look for the exact moment when the feeling is powerful. In this exact moment, careful probing can open up or access a newfound, newly discovered, hidden, deeper way of experiencing, a deeper way of being, an inner deeper person.

The exact moment for the boy is when his father bursts into utter sobbing. Careful probing inside this moment accesses an inner deeper potential for experiencing incredible closeness and melding intimate fusion with his father, a warm oneness. For the woman, the exact moment of powerful feeling is when the drunken neighbor is pawing and grabbing her body. Careful probing into this exact moment yielded a whole new, inner, deeper experiencing of viciousness, cruelty, and menacing violence.

Step 2. Give the person plenty of opportunity to welcome, to appreciate, to enjoy, and to feel good about the discovered, hidden, deeper potential for experiencing. He is able to savor and to treasure the inner, deeper closeness and melding intimate fusion, this warm oneness. She welcomes the inner, deeper experiencing of being able to be vicious, cruel, and menacingly violent. In this step, the purpose is to use whatever methods enable the person to relate well toward, to come to welcome and accept, to cherish, what had been hidden, sealed off, and kept down.

Step 3. Show the person how to transform into actually being and behaving as this whole new person in the context of earlier life scenes. Start by finding a number of earlier life scenes, including those from relatively recent times, some years ago, and some from early childhood. One way is to start with the deeper experiencing: "Just see whatever times come to mind when you think of viciousness, cruelty, and menacing violence." She has flashes of several earlier incidents. One is when she was about four years old and bit her uncle's finger, and he slapped her face so hard that she cried profusely.

Another way to find earlier life scenes is by using the general contours of the scene from Step 1: "Just see whatever times come to mind when you think of someone telling you something awful, shocking, and terrible." He recollects several times. One is when he was about 12 years old, and a leering buddy said that he had sex with the patient's younger sister.

In each of the earlier life scenes, the person is to live and be as the qualitatively new person and, importantly, is to do so within a liberating context of absolutely playful unreality. She now reacts to the uncle's slap by being the whole new girl who is the energized essence of full-bore viciousness, cruelty, and menacing violence. He transforms into being the whole new person who showers his acquaintance, his younger sister, and everyone else with cascading warm closeness and melding intimate fusion. Both patients are completely new persons in these and other earlier life scenes, and all within a context of sheer playfulness, unreality, rollicking fun, and zaniness.

Step 4. Being the qualitatively new person in the new real world after the session. The aim of this step is to enable the qualitatively new person to get a taste of what it is like to live and be in the new real world of tomorrow and beyond.

Find all sorts of scenes and situations from tomorrow and the next few days or so, scenes and situations that are forthcoming or that can be concocted in sheer fantasy, scenes and situations that are cordial to this whole new person as well as those that are shockingly inappropriate and even grossly antagonistic.

Then the person is to hurl himself or herself into being this qualitatively new person in all of these forthcoming scenes and situations, but within the freeing context of absolutely playful unreality, hilarity, fantasy, comedy, unconstrained madness, and silliness. She transforms into being galloping viciousness, cruelty, and menacing violence as she wakes up tomorrow, as she drives to work, with her family, in the committee meeting on Wednesday, and in sexual play with her favorite lover. He converts into a hilarious, loving, caring, and incredibly close melding intimate fusion with his father-in-law at church this Sunday, at the grave of his deceased grandmother a few days hence, and with his boss in the large department meeting tomorrow.

Then you move toward reality. By means of a back-and-forth interplay of rehearsal, modification of what seems fitting, checking and trying it out, and seeing what strikes good and bad chords the patients settle on how to be this whole new way in appropriate scenes and in fitting ways. After much rehearsal, she is ready to revel in a delightful sense of good-feelinged viciousness, cruelty, and menacing violence in guiding her boyfriend through dangerously exciting new sexual games, with his conjoining cooperation of course. For his part, he arrived at a commitment to be alone with his father, something he rarely did, and to find out more about his father's own childhood, something he had done almost never, with all of this coming from and allowing for a new-felt sense of loving, caring, incredible closeness and melding intimate oneness with his father.

In one session, both persons gained a remarkable taste and sample of being a qualitatively new person, each in his and her own way, each wound around something deeper inside and being free of his and her compelling scenes of bad feeling. You are invited to follow the four steps as a way of attaining these two transformational objectives in a single session of experiential psychotherapy.

MEMORY COLLAGE

Therapists: Jean Marnocha, M.S.W., & Beth Haasl, B.S.

Affiliation: Jean Marnocha is an Independent Clinical Social Worker and Beth Haasl is a Grief Counselor. Both currently are affiliated with Unity Hospice, a community hospice program in Green Bay, Wisconsin.

Major work:
> Haasl, B., & Marnocha, J. (1990). *Bereavement support group program for children*. Muncie, IN: Accelerated Development. (Editor's Note: This work is available in a "Leader Manual" for use with ages 5 to 15 and a "Participant Workbook" for use with ages 7 through 15.)

Population for whom the technique is appropriate: This activity is used in our children's grief group program, which is held for children of kindergarten age to 15 years old. This activity also could be adapted for use with adults.

Cautionary notes: None.

This technique, described in our own leader's manual referenced above, is adapted from an activity in *Thanatopics: A Manual of Structured Learning Experience for Death Education* (1982), by Eugene J. Knott and Mary C. Ribar, entitled "Death Collage."

Purpose

Using this technique may be a helpful way for children to cope with grief in a positive way. It offers children the opportunity to explore the use of memories as a positive way in which to deal with grief. Discussing memories in this way gives children the chance to talk about the special and memorable qualities of their loved one who has died, in a non-threatening environment.

Activity Method

Warm-up. In order to assist children in beginning to recall thoughts of their loved one who died, a warm-up activity is helpful. Reading a book such as, *The Tenth Good Thing about Barney*, by Judith Viorst (1987), may facilitate discussion about memories. The importance of sharing memories should be stressed, even though remembering is sometimes painful.

Memory Sharing. Each individual has been asked to bring to the session a memory object that they share and talk about. Questions that will stimulate reminiscence may be asked by group members. Examples of some questions are the following: Why is this important? Where is this memory object kept? Is this something that you did together? Are there other memories you would like to share?

Constructing the Memory Collage. (Materials needed: pencils, markers, magazines that can be cut up, scissors, and paste or glue.) Pass out a large piece of construction paper, scissors, glue or paste, and magazines. Ask participants to find pictures in magazines of things that serve as reminders of their loved ones who have died, such as foods, hobbies, and interests. Have them cut out the pictures and paste them on the construction paper to form a collage. The counselor or co-counselors can facilitate memories using examples of magazine pictures as triggers for the group members. Drawing or writing about memories may be used to further describe the memory collages. After they have completed their collages, ask participants to share them with the group.

References

Knott, E., & Ribar, M. C. (1982). *Thanatopics: A manual of structured learning experience for death education.* Encinitas, CA: SLE Publications.

Viorst, J. (1987). *The tenth good thing about Barney.* New York: Macmillan.

THERAPEUTIC ASSESSMENT

Therapist: Scott T. Meier, Ph.D.

Affiliation: State University of New York (SUNY) Buffalo; private practice.

Major works:
> Meier, S. T. (1994). *The chronic crisis in psychological measurement and assessment.* New York: Academic Press.
> Meier, S., & Davis, S. (1993). *The elements of counseling* (2nd ed.). Pacific Grove, CA: Brooks/Cole.

Population for whom the technique is appropriate: Counselor's discretion.

Cautionary notes: None.

My counseling experience and reading of the research literature have convinced me of the importance of integrating assessment into the counseling process. Currently, there is considerable interest in outcome assessment on the part of individual counselors, insurance companies, and professional organizations. While some of that interest results from an emphasis on cost containment, assessment procedures also can help counselors evaluate the ideas we hold about how best to help our clients. That is, all therapists develop a set of ideas and relations among those ideas (i.e., case conceptualization) about what is troubling their clients and what they could be doing to help them. Formally evaluating those concepts through assessment can help guide counselors through the therapeutic process.

The technique described herein combines elements from behavioral assessment and psychometric approaches. The first step in this assessment-intervention process is to develop a graphic model of the change process for a specific client. The two most basic elements of the model are the *process* and the *outcome* components. With any particular client, we can describe his or her issues in terms of processes that lead to a set of outcomes. We can identify these elements, for example, on the basis of our knowledge of psychotherapy theories, past experiences with similar clients, supervisors' and colleagues' feedback, and so forth. In general, we are seeking the simplest model possible, based on some theory, that can help us understand a particular client.

We then can attempt to operationalize those processes and outcome elements for the purpose of collecting quantitative and qualitative data about the client. Particularly for outcome measures, we can rely on previously published scales such as the *Global Assessment of Functioning* (GAF) *Scale* in the American Psychiatric Association's *Diagnostic and Statistical Manual* (DSM). But with many clients, a more individualized approach may be useful. From the graphic model, define all process and outcome constructs, elaborating on their key components with the specific client. Note typical examples of the construct as well as questionable instances. Next, define the response dimensions you will record, and then begin collecting data.

Once we have some data, we can begin to evaluate the model we initially constructed. The simplest analysis is to plot a time series of data collected over time and session. With outcome measures, we can examine whether trends are apparent in the desired directions (e.g., symptom decrease). We may decide that the assessments of the elements of the model are flawed and require modification as well. For example, we might decide to modify the GAF because it is not assessing problems in more specific domains (e.g., interpersonal, occupational, and intrapsychic). We also are likely to find that the model needs modification. For example, we may find that behavioral interventions decrease symptoms in interpersonal and occupational domains (e.g., fewer arguments and absences), but intrapsychic symptoms (e.g., anxiety) remain high. As therapy proceeds, we repeat this process, drawing a richer, more accurate map of the processes influencing the outcomes concerning this particular client.

A brief example may help illustrate this method. KP was a single, 40-year-old woman who presented with complaints about depression, anxiety, confusion, and periodic heavy alcohol consumption. She reported that her father had been alcoholic and that she had a history of conflicted relationships with men. My initial process-outcome model indicated that her symptoms resulted from her attempts to rehabilitate important men in her life and the conflict that resulted. As the therapeutic relationship developed and the client reported more information, new constructs were added and/or substituted in the process-outcome model: her tendency to shift chaotically between total detachment and total immersion in relationships with men; her awareness that she could put limits on what she could give in relationships; her alcohol consumption; her strong self-criticism; and her sensitivity to shameful experience, both in terms of her angry reactions and her feelings of vulnerability to angry men. As KP became practiced and confident in her ability to set reasonable limits on others' demands, assessments of heavy drinking incidents decreased, she increasingly came to therapy sessions on time, and the therapist ratings of her functioning converged toward transient or mild symptoms on occupational and interpersonal activities. Assessing this client as therapy progressed enabled me to manage the complexity of the information she presented and create a useful treatment plan that led to a successful outcome.

CREATING SPA IN COUNSELING

Therapist: Richard C. Nelson, Ph.D.

Affiliation: Counselor educator, Purdue University, West Lafayette, Indiana.

Major works:
> Nelson, R. C. (1990). *Choice awareness: A systematic, eclectic counseling theory.* Minneapolis, MN: Educational Media Corporation.
> Nelson, R. C. (1992). *On the CREST: Growing through effective choices.* Minneapolis, MN: Educational Media Corporation.
> Nelson, R. C., Dandeneau, C. J., & Schrader, M. K. (1994). *Working with adolescents: Building effective communication and choice-making skills.* Minneapolis, MN: Educational Media Corporation.
> Author of five novels for young people with supplements that are designed to promote better choices.

Population for whom the technique is appropriate: Clients of any age or with any problem focus.

Cautionary notes: None.

Spa in Counseling

The process of spa in counseling is often heavy, and when serious issues have been explored, clients may leave the counseling office with a sigh, expecting that the same matter will be considered in their next session. *Spa in counseling* (Nelson, 1990, 1992) suggests that toward the end of each interview, the counselor spend from two to five minutes helping clients move toward an optimistic frame of mind as they reenter the world of others. Further, once the issue at hand has been resolved in some way, it may be advantageous to arrange follow-up interviews in which the client might share his or her successes in using the ideas developed through the counseling process.

Parallel to Spa in the Physical Domain

The term *spa* is used currently in the physical domain to mean "taking the waters" of mineral springs and engaging in exercises designed to promote a pleasant, relaxing feeling that follows the vigorous expenditure of energy.

Similarly, spa in counseling is used to focus on dialogue and activities that allow clients to "bathe" in their strengths and engage in activities that can send them away with a pleasant, relaxed feeling about themselves. Physical spa experiences are rewarding because they may clarify the need for developing additional skills or for maintaining suitable body weight, for example. Counseling-as-spa experiences are also both pleasurable and fun—even though they may clarify the need for solving additional problems, for gaining interpersonal skills, or for achieving an improved self-view.

Content of Counseling as Spa

In counseling-as-spa, counselors encourage clients to share the joyful experiences and the everyday events of their lives, help them reinforce themselves for their gains, encourage them to find the strength they need to face their struggles, and support them as they reach toward their goals. Four examples of activities follow.

Things I Can Do

"Most counseling clients see their worst side, dwell on the qualities they do not like in themselves, focus on what they cannot do or be, and in general express uncertainty about their own good qualities. The is not a good way, as the saying goes, to run a railroad" (Nelson, 1992, p. 215). "Things I Can Do" is an activity designed to help clients see their assets clearly.

After suggesting to your client that it would be good for the two of you to take a few moments to focus on his or her assets, take out a bold, bright felt pen and head a page with the title of this activity. Begin with the simplest action of all to make it clear that simple, everyday skills are suitable for the list; print the word *breathe* as the first item. Then build a list of simple, everyday things the client is able to do. Feel free to add items you are aware of, but try to elicit most of the ideas from the client. Encourage the client to savor each idea and to feel a sense of joy, of spa, about his or her capabilities, and to consider what it would be like if he or she *couldn't* do one or more of the things on the list. The list may include such items as eat, sleep, read, write, talk, walk, run, think, drive, work, dream, plan, telephone, add, subtract, multiply, divide, and cook (or boil) water. The client may carry away the page, add to it from time to time, and share the expanded list with you as a brief spa activity in one or more future sessions. This activity should offer a partial antidote to self-criticism that the client may be inclined to emphasize.

Enjoying Choices: My Favorite Things

Choice Awareness Theory (Nelson, 1990) posits five kinds of choices whose initial letters form the acronym CREST: Caring, Ruling, Enjoying, Sorrowing, and Thinking/Working. Each of the five choices offers numerous opportunities for spa experiences, especially *enjoying choices*. One example of a brief enjoying choice activity is suggested in a song from the musical, *The Sound of Music*. Invite the client to alternate with you in building a short list of "My Favorite Things." A few examples from the song of that name may be used to initiate the list: "raindrops on roses," "warm woolen mittens," "bright copper kettles," and "wild geese that fly with the moon on their wings." Building the list should elicit a few smiles, and, as above, the client may be encouraged to take away the list, add to it, and reflect on "My Favorite Things" whenever life is a bit too heavy.

A Scene That Can Bring Me Peace

A brief fantasy can help clients reenter the everyday world with a more positive mindset than they might have otherwise. Invite the client to close his or her eyes and imagine boarding and being transported away on a magic carpet to a beautiful, peaceful place. Offer two or three scenes in the fantasy, visualizing the arrival process and the setting in copious detail—a mountainside with a gurgling stream and the pleasant chirping of birds, a lake side view from the porch of a cozy cottage, a warm day and a farmhouse and red barn beside a field of plowed earth. Ask the client to take over the fantasy and describe "A Scene That Can Bring Me Peace," which may resemble one of the scenes you have described or may offer a very different view. After a few moments, ask the client to open his or her eyes and talk about why he or she sees the scene as peaceful. Encourage the client to reenact the magic carpet process and being transported to the scene of his or her choosing whenever life seems to bear in too strongly. Mention that closing one's eyes can be inappropriate at times, for example, while driving a car or operating other machinery, but even with open eyes one can picture a peaceful scene and feel a greater sense of peace.

Which Track?

Mini-spa experiences may include the use of a variety of graphics intended to bring a smile to the face of the client while pointing up the nature of the problem or a direction for the future. In "Which Track" (Nelson, 1987), the counselor draws a rudimentary sketch of a train about to approach a divide; one direction leads to trouble on a track labeled OD (for overdone choices),

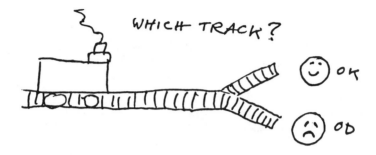

Figure 3.5.   Example of sketch for "Which Track?"

and the other leads to positive outcomes on the OK track. The sketch should help clarify for the client the two major options available. (See Figure 3.5.)

Summary

With a little thought, effective counselors may envision many additional ways of promoting positive feelings in their clients particularized for their individual needs. For those who cannot imagine alternative spa experiences, the references below may be useful; they offer additional activities and discussion of the Choice Awareness system, the basis for the concept of spa in counseling.

References

Nelson, R. C. (1987). Graphics in counseling. *Elementary School Guidance and Counseling, 22*(1), 17-29.

Nelson, R. C. (1990). *Choice awareness: A systematic, eclectic counseling theory.* Minneapolis: Educational Media Corporation.

Nelson, R. C. (1992). Spa in counseling. *Journal of Counseling and Development, 71*(2), 214-220.

SUPPORT AND CHALLENGE: USE OF METAPHOR AS A HIGHER LEVEL EMPATHIC RESPONSE

Therapist: Edward Neukrug, Ed.D.

Affiliation: Associate Professor of Counseling and Human Services; Licensed Professional Counselor and Psychologist; Old Dominion University, Norfolk, Virginia.

Major works:
> Neukrug, E. S. (1994). *Theory, practice and trends in human services: An overview of an emerging profession.* Pacific Grove, CA: Brooks/Cole.
> Neukrug, E. S. (in press). *The world of counseling: An introduction to the field* (tentative title). Pacific Grove, CA: Brooks/Cole.
> Researcher of constructive development and its relationship to education of the helping professional.

Population for whom the technique is appropriate: This technique is effective with a wide range of clients; nevertheless, it would not work with those who have moderate mental retardation. It works less well with concrete thinkers (they don't "get" the metaphor).

Cautionary notes: See above.

This technique is based on a combination of Rogerian concepts and developmental stage movement. It assumes that clients can assimilate and eventually accommodate confrontations to their existing way of viewing the world if they are challenged by the helper's use of metaphor or analogy when showing higher level empathic understanding. Since a higher level empathic response is one in which the helper reflects meaning and feelings to the client of which he or she is not fully aware, these reflections can have a profound effect on the client's understanding of self. One manner in which these higher level empathic responses can be made is through the use of metaphor. Since these responses tend to be very powerful for the client, it is usually best to use them sparingly, at peak moments in the counseling process.

Crucial to the use of metaphor as a higher level empathic response is the nature of the helping relationship. If the relationship is not supportive, nurturing, and caring, any challenge, to the client's world view, as subtle as it may be, will not be incorporated into the client's existing construction of reality. If the relationship is supportive, however, the client will practically invite the helper to offer him or her new ways of making sense of his or her world.

One example of such a response is the following. Imagine you have been working with a client and he has shared his struggles for change with you. He is in a good amount of anguish over his life's situation and has continued to try to make change, to no avail. He seems to go from one self-help group to another, one method of change to another, with limited progress. You say to him "Sounds like you are rearranging chairs on the Titanic." This response can be profound for the client because it offers a mental image of what appears to be actually happening in his life—that no matter what he does, he still is sinking. Acknowledging this can be crucial for the client to begin to understand himself in a new way. For instance, as he takes in this response, he might understand that his attempts at change appear futile. He may decide on a new approach. For instance, he may decide to try to accept himself for who he is and stop the continual efforts at the change process—for they do not seem to be working for him.

Or imagine another client, a woman who has been battered for years by her husband. She has shared the torment and the pain with you, and yet she continues to go back to the abusive situation. You say to her "You know, this situation of yours sounds like a horrible movie. It has moments that are interesting, but overall it's dreadful, and yet you keep going back to it thinking it's going to have a different ending." This response could help bring a realization to the client—a realization that she already knows on some level—that, despite all the evidence that her husband will not change, *she* continues to put herself in an abusive situation. She cannot change the movie, but she can stop going to it. She cannot change her husband, but she can stop herself from being in the situation.

If in the actual offering of the response to the client, the helper finds that the client is denying or disagreeing with the metaphor, then chances are the helper did not use it at the correct moment or misunderstood the client's world view. In this case, it is important that the counselor retreat from the response, reexamine whether or not the relationship is indeed supportive enough for the client to have heard the response, and examine whether or not the response was "on target."

Although metaphors work well in making these responses, one also can use analogies or imagery, or simply provide the client with content and feelings to which they were not previously aware. All work well; however, I have found metaphors to be the most creative way for me to make these dramatic responses.

As noted earlier, timing of this response is crucial. First, you need to have a strong supportive relationship with your client. Next, the metaphor should subtly challenge the client's existing view of the world. You are virtually moving the client to a new way of viewing his or her existence. If the supportive relationship is not in place, the client is likely to reject your subtle challenge. If there is a nurturing, supportive relationship in place, the client is more likely to fully take in the response you gave and consider avenues for change. I have found that, at times, even though I am convinced that my response was "on target," my client has rebuked its offering. It is at these moments that I find I need to withdraw and fight back my inclination to argue with the client about its "rightness." When I do withdraw and attempt to make basic listening and empathic responses, I often find that my client will revisit the metaphor at a later point in the helping relationship. At this later point, the client usually finds the metaphor revealing, and the client is generally then open to the multiple meanings that the metaphor holds. When I find myself fighting with the client over its appropriateness, however, I almost always see a deterioration of the relationship. Of course, it is always best to offer the metaphor at a time that is ripe for the client—a time in which the client will accept it fully.

SOCIAL THERAPY

Therapist: Fred Newman, Ph.D.

Affiliation: Therapist; playwright; theatre director; Director of Training, East Side Institute for Short Term Therapy; staff, East Side Center for Social Therapy; Artistic Director, Castillo Cultural Center, New York.

Major works:
> Newman, F. (1994). *Let's develop! A guide to continuous personal growth.* New York: Castillo International.
>
> Newman, F. (1996). *Performance of a lifetime: A practical-philosophical guide to the joyous life.* New York: Castillo International.
>
> Newman, F., & Holzman, L. (1997). *Unscientific psychology: A cultural performatory approach to understanding human life.* Westport, CT: Praeger.
>
> Author of several other books.

Population for whom the technique is appropriate: Everyone—women and men, children and adults of every ethnicity and from all walks of life (regardless of age, "presenting problem," or prior diagnosis).

Cautionary notes: None

Social therapy is a practical, non-diagnostic and non-interpretive, short-term method for helping people re-initiate their emotional development through performance. The social therapeutic approach thereby challenges, in practice, the assumptions of knowledge-based, problem-oriented, anti-developmental psychology—including most forms of psychotherapy. Contrary to conventional psychological wisdom, there are no natural limits to human development. Over the last 25 years of practice, moreover, we have discovered that development is the cure for emotional pain and psychopathology.

By performance we mean the uniquely human activity of going beyond yourself, being someone other than who you are, and creating who you are by being who you are not. Picture the tragically common scene of a man who is storming around the house in a rage; he is going to hit his wife. That man is unself-consciously acting out the role of an abusive husband, which he has acquired in learning how to behave like a man. Crucial to that role is the assumption that when he is angry or upset, he has no choice except to hit her. But he does. He has the capacity to perform as who he is not; in that moment when he is about to hit his wife, he can tell a joke or sing a song instead. Or he can meow like a cat. He can ham it up in the style of the late comedian Jackie Gleason, as Ralph Kramden: "One of these days, Alice . . . Pow! Right in the kisser!" Or he can take his wife's hand. In doing one of these things (or any other performance), he can change the form of his anger—and of his life.

Every human being has this remarkable capacity to perform. For example, babies babble long before they know how to speak or even that there is such a thing as speaking. Adults and older children respond to the funny noises the little ones make not by judging how they do it or insisting that they be quiet until they can do it right. It is not a "problem" that these inexperienced speakers have a very limited vocabulary or that they make grammatical mistakes. Babies babble, we talk back to them, they imitate the sounds we make—not like the mimicry of parrots and monkeys, but creatively—and before we know it, they are speaking.

In other words, human beings develop as speakers by participating in a social ensemble whose members create a performance of speaking together. If very young children were not supported to perform in this way, none of us ever would make the developmental leap from baby talk to the real thing.

Early on, however, most of us are discouraged from performing; we are allowed only to be who we already are, as societally defined. Children of four or five, or even younger, are told (or warned) to "behave"—that is, to stop performing and do what the societal roles and rules require. There is nothing wrong with societal roles and roles; behavior—the infinite number of acts that get you through the day without your having to give them much thought—may be quite convenient and efficient for mailing a letter or buying groceries. But precisely because it is unself-conscious and unthinking, behavior can be enormously painful, stifling, or non-developmental when it comes to being intimate with someone you love, dealing with physical pain and illness, or handling a crisis.

This is where performance comes in. In contrast to behavior, performance is creative and self-conscious; it is how people create choices as to who, and how, they want to be. And it turns out that performance, which is how development is initiated in the first place, is how adults can continuously create their development throughout life.

The social therapy group is a performatory environment in which people are supported to create new emotional forms of life. The social therapist does not possess the true interpretation or explanation of why a client feels the way he or she feels, or does what he or she does—an underlying truth that the client must come to understand in order to solve the problem. The social therapist is more like a theatre director who helps the client create, along with other people, new performances of affection, anger, anxiety, depression, desire, excitement, grief, happiness, humiliation, impotence, panic, etc.—new forms of emotional life.

This is how performance enables people to give expression to the choices that they make and at the same time to see that they are capable of making choices. It is this self-conscious activity of continuously producing who and how you are in the world that is what we mean by development—and how development is the cure.

GAINING RAPPORT AND A COMMON BASE
OF UNDERSTANDING: DEFINING RATIONAL REALITY
ON WHICH TO BUILD THROUGH COUNSELING

Therapist: Donald L. Peters, M.Ed.

Affiliation: Retired school counselor with 35 years experience at the junior high and high school levels; National President of the American School Counselor Association, 1970-1971.

Major works:
> Peters, D. L. (1967). *For thinking teens.* New York: Richards Rosen.
> Peters, D. L. (1975). *For the time of your life.* New York: Richards Rosen.
> Peters, D. L. (1991). *Counseling kids.* Muncie, IN: Accelerated Development.
> Author of other books and articles in journals and magazines.

Population for whom the technique is appropriate: Middle school through high school, but valid with all ages.

Cautionary notes: Adapt to the circumstances and the styles of the counselor and the counselee.

Introduction

Assert that ours is a *fun oriented* society—whether dealing with drug abuse (prevention or treatment), career planning, counterproductive sexual behaviors, or whatever. Then, interacting with the counselee, try to get at what we mean by *fun.* Suggest that there are seven basic ingredients—whether we are talking about a brief activity or the totality of a person's life. What unfolds is that our consideration of these seven areas of basic need may be seen as a valid, productive approach in both group work and individual counseling. At the very least, this offers a collection of headings with which to explore problems and seek solutions.

An Example—Drug Use

When viewing how and why people get into using drugs, consider the following:

Action. Drug use is something to do. It fills a void for some and is a substitute for boredom. For many, it is where the action is. Drug use often is linked to considerable enabling, preparatory, and ritualistic activity.

Discovery. Drug use provides learning and discovery experiences in finding out the feelings resulting from ingestion, in supposed self-discovery with use of "mind expanding" drugs, and in the social and sexual experiences of the scene.

Emotional Experience. Drugs offer fabulous feelings. They are ingested in the quest to feel better and gain a high. Some users see drugs as "frosting on the cake" to make excitement and good times even better. Some see drug dependency as a love affair complete with orgasmic experience far superior to the sexual variety. For some, the risk-taking does not deter but enhances the excitement of it all.

Belonging. Drugs are ingested by some because it seems "everyone is doing it," and it is a requirement of the crowd in order to belong. Drugs are used by others in somewhat different circumstances to cope with loneliness and the lack of belonging, to counter the depressions of rejection.

Voice. Young people tend to see drug use as an assertion of independence and a symbol of rebellion against authority. Some use drugs to exercise voice in their own affairs and some to defy parents, school, and the established community.

Being Somebody. Many see their drug experience as self-elevating. They see themselves as significant somebodies because of their association with the drug scene. Both because of the drug-induced feelings and because of the esoteric creations of the media and other profiting enterprises, many see drug use as necessary to really be somebody.

The Look Ahead. Drug use offers temporary escape from the depression of a dismal, threatening, empty look ahead—a look ahead to First Period, tonight, tomorrow, or 10 years down the line. For many, alcohol and drugs provide something to look forward to, something wonderful within reach, an invitation to party and feeling better, no matter how poor the grades, how rotten things many be at home, or how dark and pointless the future.

When seeking fun, as prevention or treatment, or simply with the goal of the good life, the answers can be found in well-rounded activities that

1. keep people in *action*—physically and/or mentally;
2. offer opportunities for *discovery* and *learning*;
3. provide genuine *emotional experiences*;

4. foster a feeling of *belonging;*
5. permit people to have a *voice* in what they do;
6. recognize people as significant *somebodies*; and
7. give consideration to the *look ahead*, both in avoiding regrettable happenings and in leading toward happy, worthwhile things to come.

An oversimplification, indeed. Uniquely individual, personal problems can interfere with a person's capacity to have fun. And catastrophic world events surely can put a damper on what can be. But even in the more complex situations, keeping these seven areas of need in mind can help.

The fact is, when things are a bit on the complicated side, it is especially important to apply rational concepts with which to think and to consider situations point by point in terms that are understood by those involved—*one step at a time.*

To me, a certain thrill continues in using this formula as a guide in counseling. So simple it can be, yet so effective in getting at what is happening and why, and in moving toward making things better all around.

WALLY THE WORRYING WARTHOG

Therapist: Janie J. Plaxco, M.A.

Affiliation: Licensed Counselor in private practice.

Major work:
   Plaxco, J. (1994). *Helping friends: A helping book for kids who have been sexually abused.* Tuscaloosa, AL: Plaxco.

Population for whom the technique is appropriate: Young children up to early adolescence.

Cautionary notes: None

In my 10 years experience in counseling, I have worked with children with many types of problems. Two populations on which I have focused are child survivors of sexual abuse and children whose parents have divorced. Given the multitude and magnitude of feelings and worries these children often face, I have found it is often quite difficult to get them to acknowledge and deal with what is bothering them. "Wally" makes this step a lot easier for the kids. Plus, he's a lot of fun!

Children have taught me two basic things:

1. Kids would much rather have "worries" than "problems." While the word "problem" seems to infer internal fault/blame, "worry" indicates external responsibility. I have asked children about problems and have been told they have none. Yet when asked about worries, they often readily list several. We never discuss "problems" in my office anymore, only "worries."
2. Children need boundaries. Once, in a group for latency age children of divorce, we were talking about court and child support. As I was trying to explain the two concepts, one child interrupted me and said, "Janie, that's grown-up stuff." Nearly every child I work has been constantly reminded, "Kids don't need to worry about grown-up stuff; kids only need to worry about kids' stuff."

To get to the worries, to remind kids about the difference between grown-up and kid stuff, and to add to the fun of coming to see me, Wally agreed to come work with me. Wally is actually a poster of a green monster published by

Carson and Dellosa and is readily available from school supply stores. He's great! He loves kids and has several hanging around him. He loves fried chicken—the kids have a giant drumstick for him. He gets his teeth brushed by one mouse while another is telling him a joke in his ear. The best part is that he has HUGE teeth. This is great because sometimes you might need to call him into your nightmares, and he needs to look *real scary* (although you know he really isn't) to scare off all the bad guys. Wally also has only three fingers, so, since he can't write very well, he has to type his letters. He seems to come into my office when I'm not there and writes letters to the kids on my computer.

Wally is introduced to a child during our first session. I explain that Wally is a very cool guy who's crazy about kids and wants to help kids with their worries. His job is worrying, because even though it is hard to imagine, he *loves* to worry! (By this time, most kids are hooked.) I then explain that Wally and I have a rule: "Kids don't need to worry about grown-up stuff; kids *only* need to worry about kid stuff." When kids have grown-up worries, they can leave them for Wally, and he will write them back a letter. The kids are reminded that they are not supposed to worry about something if Wally is worrying about it. He wants them to worry about kid stuff like school and playing. Older kids write their own worries. Younger kids dictate to me, after I explain that I won't listen because this is just between Wally and them but that I will write it for them. The child then is instructed to fold the letter so nobody can see it but Wally. The letter then is taped to Wally.

It is essential, of course, that you never forget to write the letters to the kids. Often I have kids coming in next session looking at Wally first thing for their letter. Once or twice, Wally went to the beach or on vacation (I'd forgotten to write the letter back!), but when that happened, he wrote them an extra special letter and mailed it to their home. Parents often report that the kids will check the daily mail in anticipation of a letter from Wally.

Wally has secured details of sexual abuse that I had been trying to get for several sessions. Kids have expressed feelings to him that they haven't felt comfortable expressing to me. In his letters back, Wally always thanks the child for the letter and comments on how very big the worry was. He comments on how much he and I enjoy knowing the kid. He then talks some about the worry, but mostly refers the child to me, explaining that I like to help kids, that I'm a friend of his, and that he thinks I might have some good ideas. With children who have been sexually abused, he often identifies us as part of the child's "team" or group of people who care about and protect the child. He is always careful to remind the child to try to worry about kid stuff only and that whenever the child worries about grown-up stuff to let a grown-up know.

I'm right-handed and sign the letters with my left hand. Wally can't write very well since he has only three fingers. The children often want to take their letters home, but sometimes they want to leave them with me in their charts to look over from time to time. Sometimes children figure out that I write the letters and that there is no *real* Wally. I then explain that Wally is pretend, but he's awfully fun. These children invariably write more letters.

The primary goal of Wally is to offer additional support and encourage the child to trust and talk with me. He is a springboard to discussion, ventilation of feelings, problem-solving, and basic coping skill building. The object is really not to have Wally solve any problems, but rather to have him offer ideas that you and the child can discuss.

This technique can be used with stuffed animals or other posters. I would advise that whatever you use should have the potential to be quite *mean* to offer the protection the child might need. For example, I have a 20-foot long stuffed green snake, Sally, who also gets some letters. Not only do Wally and Sally making counseling more fun, they often come up with ideas I had not thought of and they are excellent company for me while I'm doing paperwork!

DEALING WITH SILENCE: THE TURTLE ANALOGY FOR PSYCHOTHERAPISTS AND COUNSELORS

Therapist: John E. Poarch, M.D., F.A.P.A.

Affiliation: Board Certified Psychiatrist; Clinical Professor of Psychiatry, University of Oklahoma Health Sciences Center; private practice.

Major work:
> Poarch, J. E. (1990). *Limits: The keystone of emotional growth.* Muncie, IN: Accelerated Development.

Population for whom the technique is appropriate: Silent clients.

Cautionary notes: None.

Mothers and their babies communicate feelings empathically before the infant learns words. The messages are very accurate. All of us know that a cry can mean many different things (e.g., anger, sadness, distress, or exercise of heart, lungs, and muscle since infants can not jog). Toddlers are notoriously responsive and expressive of a parent's anxiety. Unfortunately, most of use learn to distort our communication with words.

Nearly 30 years ago as a resident in psychiatry, I saw a 14-year-old, inpatient schizophrenic boy three times each week for one year. Nearly all the sessions were excruciatingly silent. For me, the hours were miserable because I felt that I was not doing anything helpful. Every moment reinforced my fears and feelings of inadequacy. Early on, my comments and questions, geared only to elicit speech, were met with reticence and, when I tried too hard, hostility. Minutes were eons of very painful doubt and uncertainty. At times, it seemed that even my worry and concern were met with a negative response.

I later learned that all my energies were overprotective and did not treat my patient as though he were his own, capable person. I was being just like his mother and father, both of whom I met with weekly.

Over the years, I have had occasion to see many silent patients. I also have supervised the treatment of innumerable others. Spouses often complain of an uncommunicative partner and parents of taciturn offspring. I have found the analogy of a turtle to be extremely useful in treating the patient, in supervision, and in helping spouses and parents with this perplexing dilemma.

If we imagine the patient as a turtle in a tightly closed shell, certainly we would make no verbal efforts to get the turtle to come out knowing that any effort would make the turtle squeeze the shell more tightly. We learn in time that even if we are spending energy in our minds trying to contrive a way to induce the patient to open up, the patient empathically senses this and remains mute. If the therapist ignores the shell and insists on pressing, the result can be violence during or immediately after the session. I have had that occur.

When the patient does begin to speak, the therapist may mistakenly read his or her excitement as something other than empathic communication from the patient. By this I mean that if the therapist experiences his or her satisfaction as independent from the patient's excitement and is pleased with self or pleased with patient rather than happy for patient, the head of the turtle is withdrawn. Odds are that the patient has become delighted at emerging from the shell, which, by nature, he or she is yearning to do. If the therapist does anything to enable the patient to talk—for example, ask questions or repeat words or phrases—the patient will, of course, pull back and become quiescent. Only if the therapist treats the patient as he or she would a turtle will the head protrude for increasing periods of time, facilitating emotional growth in the process of psychotherapy.

I want to emphatically encourage the therapist to pay attention to his or her own inner thoughts and feelings (with the thoughts to be considered as symbols or images representing feelings) as probable empathic communication from the silent patient. One then must wait for possible confirmation.

The most difficult aspect of the therapist's task is simply to tolerate the silence without asking questions to pretend one is "doing something" or making comments merely to relieve the discomfort of the silence. At this point, the odds are overwhelming that the silence is making the patient uncomfortable. On the other hand, the silence can be very pleasant, even erotic.

Sometimes the patient may get angry because the therapist does not talk or refuses to ask questions to relieve the discomfort. When this happens, I often respond, "I could do that and it would make us both more comfortable, but it would not turn out to be helpful. I then would be just an overprotective mother interfering with your growth while convincing myself that I was being helpful."

When one is having trouble always refer back to the metaphor!

OLFACTORY CONDITIONING:
THE SWEET AROMA OF POST-HYPNOTICS

Therapist: Howard G. Rosenthal, Ed.D.

Affiliation: Licensed Professional Counselor; National Certified Counselor; Certified Clinical Mental Health Counselor; Master Addictions Counselor; Program Director, Human Services, St. Louis Community College at Florissant Valley; private practice.

Major works:
> Rosenthal, H. G. (1988). *Not with my life I don't: Preventing your suicide and that of others.* Muncie, IN: Accelerated Development.
> Rosenthal, H. G. (1993). *Encyclopedia of counseling: Master review and tutorial.* Muncie, IN: Accelerated Development.
> Rosenthal, H. G., & Hollis, J. W. (1994). *Help yourself to positive mental health.* Muncie, IN: Accelerated Development.
> Author of journal articles as well as audio and video programs related to mental health and counselor licensure.

Population for whom the technique is appropriate: This strategy is often very successful in terms of eliminating panic attacks, anxiety reactions, phobias, and undesirable habits in children, adolescents, and adults.

Cautionary notes: Therapists should be trained in hypnosis or systematic desensitization prior to the implementation of this procedure. This technique never should be utilized in an attempt to abate suicidal and/or homicidal impulses.

Ms. K, a young woman of 22, consulted me concerning her four-pack-a-day smoking habit. It was literally difficult for her to catch her breath as she recounted the failures of her last three hypnotists, not to mention the ongoing self-help group she had joined three months prior to our interview. As she excused her incessant coughing, she explained that for some reason or another, her hypnotic sessions just never stayed with her when she felt the urge to smoke. My clinical intuition rapidly convinced me that something of a drastic nature would have to be implemented in order for my induction to "stay with her."

My incipient question must have hit her like a ton of bricks: "What flavor of juice do you enjoy the most?" To say that Ms. K seemed startled would be putting it mildly. "What difference does it make? Grape juice, of course."

I then explained that I would create a very special induction for her and that she should return for another appointment in 48 hours.

Prior to our next session I purchased a grape-scented lip gloss stick that had a very pungent fragrance. When Ms. K arrived, I placed her in a hypnotic trance, using a somewhat routine induction procedure. I then carefully created a scene in her mind wherein she was relaxed, not smoking, and mixing a large bowl of grape juice. While I suggested to her that she could smell the juice, I simultaneously popped open the grape-flavored lip gloss stick.

This strategy was conducted not with a sense of trickery, but rather to convince the client beyond a shadow of a doubt that the hypnosis was effective. Even more important, however, it also set the stage for my post-hypnotic, olfactory (i.e., nasal) strategy.

I continued to give her suggestions related to ameliorating her fondness for cigarette smoking and followed with a very novel post-hypnotic suggestion by dictating that each time she smelled grape, she immediately would feel relaxed and free of the urge to smoke.

After I brought her out of the trance, she praised the merits of my hypnotic technique, stating that she actually could smell the grape juice. It is noteworthy that while she was in hypnosis, I had remarked that the fragrance of grape still would be lingering after she awoke, since the lip gloss stick had left my entire office smelling like a giant bowl of grapes! Just for the record, if a client asks me if I had the stick open during the hypnosis, I feel that the only ethical thing to do is readily admit that I have. Most clients, nonetheless, never inquire, and when clients have asked, I have not noticed that this appreciably hinders the treatment process.

I explained to Ms. K that she should secure a grape flavored lip gloss stick and should smell it only when she has utilized all her willpower and still feels like lighting up a cigarette. Wording the directive in this manner helped ward off habituation that indeed will occur if the client actually wears the lip gloss or begins sniffing it too frequently.

Within three weeks' time, she referred to herself as an "ex-smoker." The olfactory sensation of grape reinstated the relaxed, positive feelings she experienced in her hypnotic sessions.

Although the purpose of this discussion is not to speculate about the theoretical underpinnings of this strategy, this technique seemingly favors Salter's

(1949) behavioristic contention that hypnosis is merely a form of classical conditioning set forth via Pavlov (1927). One could argue convincingly that the scent acts as a conditioned stimulus or perhaps gains its therapeutic power through the principle of higher-order conditioning.

For over 15 years, I personally have used this paradigm to successfully treat literally hundreds of cases involving difficulties such as smoking, drinking, weight control, nail biting, and panic disorder, to name a few.

The issue of habituation must be dealt with inasmuch as the phenomenon can render the technique useless. A client who was using her scented lip gloss stick to ward off panic attacks told me the following tale of woe. She left my office and could feel an attack coming on. She was amazed by the fact that after smelling the lip gloss stick for a matter of seconds she felt calm and relaxed, and did not experience an attack. She was so enthralled with the results that she went home and left the lip gloss stick open on her night stand while she slept so it could "really sink into her unconscious mind" as she put it. Needless to say, she was thoroughly disappointed when she became aware of an impending attack and the olfactory suggestion proved futile. On another occasion, I used the paradigm with a middle-school youngster who suffered from acute test anxiety. The technique worked for a short period of time and then appeared to be totally and completely ineffective. After questioning this youngster extensively, I was able to unravel the mystery. The young man had chosen a lip gloss stick whose fragrance was based on a popular brand of soda pop. The child sitting next to my client at lunch, just prior to the class, would routinely drink a bottle of this brand of soda each day. In cases such as these, the only therapeutic solution is to re-apply the technique using a *new* and *markedly different* fragrance.

Although Ms. K's case was successful, I must admit it was a tad atypical in the sense that I am usually much more careful to take precautions in regard to this issue. The following is a rough sketch of what I say to a client to help us ward off habituation *before* it becomes an issue.

Suggestions Given Prior to the Hypnotic Induction to Ward Off Habituation

"I want you to purchase a lip gloss stick with a fragrance you like. Make certain that it is *not* a fragrance you come in contact with every day or on a regular basis. For example, if you wear lip gloss with a given fragrance, then purposely don't pick that fragrance or something similar to it. If you chew bubble gum, then you most assuredly don't want a bubble gum lip gloss stick. If you use lemon wax on your furniture at home or at the office, then steer clear of lemon lip gloss sticks. Perhaps you have a cherry scented deodorizer in your car, truck, or van. If so, stay away from cherry. Anyway, after you purchase your lip gloss stick, I want you to smell it once or twice for a brief moment to see if you find it desirable. But only smell it for a very brief period of time—a few seconds is more than adequate—and whatever you do, *don't wear it.* In fact, if you know you like a particular fragrance, just buy it and don't even smell it. Just bring it to your next session. You don't even need to open the package or the tube."

Many clients, I might add, do indeed bring in an unopened stick, often still in its unopened packing.

Suggestions Given after the Hypnotic Induction to Ward Off Habituation

"Okay. I believe you responded very well to my hypnotic suggestions. The meter indicated that you *really* relaxed, and when I told you that your hand felt hot, the temperature obviously did increase. (Note: Unless the client protests, I hook one finger up to a portable biofeedback temperature training apparatus that provides me with visual feedback. This action allows me to monitor the client's relative degree of relaxation. Moreover, I have no doubt that the scientific-looking electronic device acts as a powerful placebo. This is especially true in the majority of cases where the client visited another professional therapist and/or hypnotist who did not utilize biofeedback equipment.)

"Now, I really don't think you are going to have any problems. Nevertheless, if you do feel like smoking (drinking alcoholic beverages, over eating, becoming panicky, becoming anxious, etc.), I want you to try to control your reaction via your own willpower and control. If and *only if* you can't control yourself, I want you to take your lip gloss stick out of your pocket/purse and smell it like this (I generally demonstrate this for the client) for just a brief moment or two and then close it. Never wear it or leave the stick open. Here's why. What happens if you are in a room with a woman who is wearing very strong perfume or a man wearing offensive cologne? I think you will agree that at first the fragrance is overpowering, but after perhaps an hour or so your body shuts down and you can't consciously smell it anymore. Presumably the human body is built this way so we can get on with our lives and not be immobilized by the overwhelming scent of this woman's outlandish perfume or this guy's outrageous cologne! (Note: With very young children who could not identify with the aforementioned analogy, I might ask, "What would happen if you ate only your favorite food at every single meal? Well, I think you'll agree that after a few meals, your favorite food would lose its taste and you wouldn't really enjoy it. In fact, you might get sick of it, wouldn't you? Your taste buds would just shut down.") The moral of the story is that your nasal passages also will shut down if you use your lip gloss stick too often. I want you to use it only as a last resort. The less you use your lip gloss stick, the better it will work. (I tell the client the story about the lady who left the stick open on her night stand.)

"If you begin to smell your lip gloss when you are not intentionally using it, then you can try putting it in a small plastic bag. If you still can detect the aroma, the only solution is to purchase a new stick with the same fragrance. It is usually best if you don't switch brands."

In rare cases in which a client refuses to be hypnotized, I want to emphasize that olfactory procedures can be combined easily with creative visualization/guided imagery sessions or used as an adjunct to supplement traditional systematic desensitization as outlined by Wolpe (1973). In the case of systematic desensitization, my recommendation would be that you pop open the lip gloss stick for brief periods of time when the client successfully conquers the final (i.e., the most anxiety-evoking item) step in the hierarchy of the desensitization in imagination without experiencing distress.

Give this strategy a whirl. I am certain you too will discover that in many instances, the sweet aroma of post-hypnotics works even when everything else has failed.

References

Pavlov, I. P. (1927). *Conditioned reflexes.* (G.V. Anrep, trans.) London: Oxford University Press.

Salter, A. (1949). *Conditioned reflex therapy.* New York: Capricorn Press.

Wolpe, J. (1973). *The practice of behavior therapy.* New York: Pergamon Press.

USING EARLY MEMORIES TO ELICIT
COMPLEMENTARITY IN COUPLES COUNSELING

Therapist: Steven Slavik, M.A.

Affiliation: Private practice in marital and individual counseling and therapy, Victoria, B.C., Canada.

Major work:
>Slavik, S., & Croake, J. W. (1995). *Psychological tolerance and mood disorders: An Adlerian integration.* Fort Coquitlam, BC: Canadian Counselling Institute.
>Author of 18 articles describing Adlerian theory and technique.

Population for whom the technique is appropriate: Couples seeking marital counseling.

Cautionary notes: This technique is not appropriate for couples if either partner satisfies criteria for DSM-IV personality disorders. Such individuals may deny or disparage an interpretation. It is not appropriate for someone who recalls an early memory of violence, even if violence is not the current issue. If the current issue is one of violence within the relationship, this technique is not appropriate. This technique also will not work well with clients who are fighting in the therapist's office or who will not stop blaming one another.

As a rule, if the therapist thinks offering an interpretation may lead to denial or will otherwise fail to be useful, he or she should not continue. Nonetheless, this technique is useful for a therapist to interpret the memory for his or her own information (Slavik, 1995). The therapist does not allow the technique to embroil him or her in being right. The therapist does not try to force a client to accept this information. The therapist learns to lose gracefully.

In general, the therapist does not interpret to clients in such a way as to further increase their discouragement. Many individuals may be overwhelmed easily with the thought, "So how do I change this?" Individual change is not always the purpose of this method. The therapist is prepared to explain that the purpose of this method is to help clarify why a couple has repetitive trouble and to help generate possibilities for help.

Introduction

The aim of couples therapy in an Adlerian perspective is to aid individuals to live together in egalitarian, cooperative relationships. The greatest enemies that equal relationships encounter are individual expectations that another will automatically act to please one, avoid doing anything one dislikes, and generally see things just as one does. A desire for superiority, expressed through these expectations, easily leads to complementary efforts of domination and resistance. One's lifestyle convictions readily justify efforts at being best, being in control, being first—in general, being dominant, no matter what specific words one uses. The only solution to such striving is to shift issues from "Who will win?" or "How can I get the other to understand what I want?" to "What can we do to improve the situation?" Only when one is interested in addressing the needs of the situation, rather than in winning, is equality established. Further, only when each partner is more interested in the other than in himself or herself will partnership be successful.

In the current focus on short-term, solution-oriented therapy, it is important to clarify difficulties that couples have in ways that are meaningful to the couple and that open options for change. The method presented here provides clarification and alternatives, and is appropriate for many couples experiencing relationship difficulties. In general, it helps partners understand how they cooperate to create problems and how they can learn to cooperate to encourage one another. While this technique is not based on the Connexions Focusing Technique described by Lew and Bettner (1993) and Bettner and Lew (1993), their accounts provide excellent background.

Through therapists' use of this method, couples can understand (a) their unconscious purposes for choosing one other, (b) how they cooperate for both good and bad, (c) why and how they misunderstand the meaning of one another's behavior in their own terms, (d) how the other partner is acting and why he or she acts as he or she does and, (e) how they may try to provoke behavior from one another that they can use to justify their own behavior and feelings (Bettner & Lew, 1993).

The Technique

The following process may take from one to several sessions. There is no advantage in hurrying it.

Step 1. The therapist encourages the couple to present their difficulty in their usual way. The only restriction placed on them is to ask each partner individually to describe how he or she sees the difficulty and what solution would suit each of them.

Step 2. The therapist tests each client's "psychological flexibility" by asking why some obvious (to the therapist) solution or compromise would not work for them. Sometimes this does work, and no further counseling is required.

Step 3. At any point after the description of the difficulty, the therapist may introduce the following technique. Its timing depends on how "psychologically flexible" the individuals appear to be. The more so, the sooner it can be introduced.

The therapist asks partner A for his or her earliest memory and writes it down verbatim. The therapist may need to clarify what is wanted. Many individuals think this is a "test" for how early they can recall. Many think "bad" experiences are being requested. Many give a "report." The therapist initially clarifies that any memory will do, so long as it happened only once. Most individuals then can recall a memory with a comment such as, "I've always remembered this one; I don't know why."

Step 4. If the therapist interprets the memory, he or she offers the explanation that "We don't recall things by accident. I believe that our earliest memories serve as examples of how life is, how others are, and how we are or are supposed to be. We may recall how life is when it goes badly or when it goes well. It sounds to me that the one you have recalled is about. . . ." The therapist then proceeds to offer a careful, sometimes tactful, summary of what the memory the individual has offered seems to say about how he or she behaves in life today. The therapist is careful to say that one is only guessing, and that confirmation is needed: "Could it be that. . . ? I'm only guessing, and I want your verification. Does this seem like you, or am I off the wall?" Most of the time one will receive some amount of verification. All of this is standard technique for using early memories (Slavik, 1991).

Step 5. The therapist discusses the meaning of the memory and guesses more if needed to make the interpretation more accurate and to get it in terms that the individual understands. It is a matter of agreement. The therapist keeps the current issue in mind when an interpretation is offered. These are two points on a line. *If the therapist cannot get agreement, he or she drops it* and does not continue this technique at this time.

Step 6. When the therapist has agreement, he or she asks the other partner for an opinion: "Do you recognize this? Is this the person you know?

Does it make any sense to you? Do you recognize that he/she does that?" The therapist does not allow blame—this a matter of cooperative, curious discussion. If the other partner does not recognize the behavior, the therapist does not press it.

Step 7. The therapist discusses this model with the client until the topic is exhausted at this time. The therapist elicits in detail how person A exhibits the behavior agreed upon. The therapist finds out in detail the circumstances in which person A acts in the way described, how person A justifies the behavior, and how behaving in that way solves some problem or did solve some problem. The therapist could suggest that "Perhaps this is why you have this issue with your partner just now?" The therapist asks about pros and cons, in particular how acting this way may "make trouble" for the client. The therapist may bring in the idea of *community* and how this behavior aids or hinders one from being useful in a community of two or a family. One respects limits; clients may never have considered any of these questions.

Step 8. At some point, not necessarily in the same session, the therapist asks person B for his or her earliest memory and goes through the same procedure.

Step 9. The Cycle. If it has not already become apparent, the discouraging cycle in which the partners participate can be clarified. It will be apparent that it is not either partner's "fault."

As Bettner and Lew (1993) have suggested, these discussions may be sufficient for some clients. The discussions that have ensued may be adequately clarifying to some, and the couple may make "spontaneous" adjustments. If not, however, the information that a therapist now has enables him or her to describe in some detail the interactions or transactions the clients have that are currently troublesome, and their motivations for those interactions.

The therapist can begin to tailor cognitive and behavioral interventions or suggest cognitive and behavioral modifications to their interactions that are extremely specific and proposed in terms that the clients themselves use.

An Example

Bill and Mary come to couples counseling at a point when they both agree life together is almost intolerable. Bill is an electrical engineer, and Mary is a housewife who has worked on and off during her marriage. When they met, she worked on a fishing boat. They have been together 20 years, but at this point their children are almost ready to leave home. Bill and Mary seem amenable to this technique.

In the first interview, it is apparent that Mary is very sensitive to criticism, and she agrees readily that others' opinions of her are very important to her. Initially she is weepy and claims to be helpless to change matters. She says that she has withdrawn emotionally and sexually from Bill. Bill, on the other hand, is blunt and little given to emotion. He is sensitive to loss of order or lack of control. He is apparently unaware of his impact on his wife. He too is at his wits' end and cannot "get" any affection (read sex) from her. Counseling could develop from this point in order to modify these attitudes. Early memories are hardly needed to clarify matters, but early recollections always help reveal the meaning of attitudes.

A Typical Early Memory from Bill. I recall walking in a single file with my brothers on a path in the snow with the snow over my head. I felt okay.

This is interpreted to Bill as "I like order; I like knowing and having my place." This made immediate sense to him, and he recounted the use of migraines, anger, and the demands of work in order to keep order around him.

An Early Memory Related by Mary. I was at the beach with my mother and brother, the only time we went. It was sunny and blue. I liked it; I felt good.

This eventually was interpreted to Mary as "I don't like constraints; I like to have open space before me." This too was immediately obvious to her. She then could relate that she is very sensitive to criticism and does not like to feel restricted in her life.

Rather than assuming that these individuals are changing or that their circumstances have changed, one can understand the ensuing cycle as part of their life together. With these attitudes, Bill and Mary very easily fall into a cycle where he is blunt; she becomes wary and cool; he becomes more blunt, critical, and demanding; and she withdraws outright. Eventually this blows over and they warm up, he is blunt again, she withdraws, and so on. Eventually they tire of this and come to a counselor.

Of course, this is only the beginning. In the following sessions, each must become aware of his or her goals and methods and the impact on one another (Slavik, 1993). They must be able to observe themselves and one another for their impact on one another. Then changes can begin, but the changes must be tailored for this given couple.

Conclusion

Quick assessment techniques can be useful in short-term therapy, especially if the therapist can offer clear, meaningful interpretations. If these interpretations can lead to interventions the value of which both partners recognize, then cooperation is benefitted. The technique suggested in this paper can offer such benefit.

References

Bettner, B. L., & Lew, A. (1993). The connexions focusing technique for couple therapy: A model for understanding lifestyle and complementarity in couples. *Individual Psychology, 49*(3 & 4), 372-391.

Lew, A., & Bettner, B. L. (1993). The connexions focusing technique for using early recollections. *Individual Psychology, 49*(2), 166-184.

Slavik, S. (1991). Early memories as a guide to client movement through life. *Canadian Journal of Counseling/Revue Canadienne de Counseling, 25*(3), 331-337.

Slavik, S. (1993). Intimacy as goal and tool in Adlerian couples therapy. *Canadian Journal of Adlerian Psychology, 23*(2), 65-78.

Slavik, S. (1995). Presenting social interest to different life-styles. *Individual Psychology, 51*(2), 166-177.

LIFE-PLAY FANTASY EXERCISE

Therapist: Robert Taibbi, M.S.W.

Affiliation: Licensed Clinical Social Worker; Region Ten Community Services Board.

Major works:
> Taibbi, B. (1995). *Clinical supervision: A four stage process of growth and discovery.* Milwaukee, WI: Families International.
> Taibbi, B. (1996). *Sitting on the edge: Pragmatism and possibilities in family therapy.* New York: Guilford.
> Author of over a hundred journal and magazine articles in areas of supervision, clinical practice, and family life.

Population for whom the technique is appropriate: Individual adults and adolescents as well as couples in couples therapy.

Cautionary notes: This strategy is useful in the early stages of therapy but only after trust and rapport are established. Clearly this technique should not be used with psychotic clients or those displaying psychotic personality features, those who are too emotionally fragile, or those with very high expectations who will feel that they have not done it right and are overly sensitive to the therapist's reaction.

This is a guided imagery exercise that is useful in gathering history from individual clients, particularly those going through changes (divorce, marital crisis, etc.), and isolating life scripts or themes. When used in couples therapy, this technique allows each partner to understand the differences between the two of them in a nonjudgmental and nondefensive manner.

Introduction

Tell the client that this is a way of gathering some information about his or her past and to see what overall themes emerge about his or her life. You will suggest various things for him or her to imagine. There is no right or wrong way to do this, and he or she can not make a mistake. "Just let yourself see what you see." Ask the client to get comfortable and close his or her eyes. Help the client relax.

Fantasy Instructions

Say slowly the words in the following instructions (points 1, 2, 3, 4, and 6).

1. Imagine yourself entering a theater where you have come to watch a play. You walk through the lobby, where a lot of people are milling around, to the seating area. You take the best seat in the house. In front of you is a large stage with a curtain drawn across it. You make yourself comfortable, and soon the rest of the audience comes in and fills the theater.
2. The house lights dim, stage lights go on, and the play is about to begin. The curtain slowly rises on the first act. We see on stage your parents, and it is sometime before you were born. Watch what the parents do, what they say, and how they feel. See if anyone else is on stage; be aware of the scenery. Watch what happens. (Give the client about 15 seconds to silently watch.)
3. The curtain comes down, and the act is over. The curtain rises on the second act. We see on stage you, and it is sometime during your early childhood. Your parents are on stage with you. Once again, watch what happens, listen to what is said, and see if anyone else is there.
4. The curtain comes down. The curtain rises on the third act. Once again, you are on stage and it is sometime during your adolescence. One of your parents is talking to you about growing up, getting married, sex, education, and careers. Listen to what he or she says; listen to what you say back. See if anyone else is there.
5. Continue in the same manner with additional scenes (up to about four more) that seem appropriate to the client's current problems (e.g., first job, scene from first marriage, death of parent), as well as a scene from the present (e.g., "The time is the present, and you and your husband are together on stage; watch what happens."), and future scenes (e.g., "The time is two years from now and you are on stage; watch what happens").
6. The curtain comes down now on the last act, and the play is over. The stage lights go off, and the house lights go on. The audience begins to file out of the theater. You get up and follow them out. As you do, you overhear the audience members talk about the play they have just seen. Listen to what they say. Be aware of how you feel about what they are saying. When you are ready, open your eyes.

Debriefing

After the client is reoriented, ask him or her to describe to you, scene by scene, what he or she saw. Ask if anything surprised him or her. If he or she had trouble visualizing, normalize (some people are too anxious, are not good visualizers, or have blocked areas in their past). If doing the exercise with a couple, have each take a turn describing his or her play.

Feedback

The first scene may say something about the parents' early marriage, often an unconscious model of how marriages should be. The difference between the first and second scene says something about the impact that the client's birth had on the family as well as serves as a summary of childhood (similar to earliest recollections). The third scene is a way of capsulizing parent's advice about life, how life should be, the shoulds that often fill our heads. The audience reaction is summary of the play; the client's reaction to their comments (e.g., "it was boring") may say something about sensitivity to opinion of others or internal critical self.

Look for patterns (e.g., someone always crying or angry, client always alone) and relationship between present and past scenes (e.g., couple fighting in present just like parents did in the first scene). Reassure the client that this is not prophesy and is just another form of information that may say something about his or her life space right now. Tell the client to reflect on it over the week but not to worry about it. If you are working with a couple, point out the similarities and learned differences.

WELL-BEING SCALE:
AN ASSESSMENT TOOL FOR CAREGIVERS

Therapist: Susan Steiger Tebb, Ph.D.

Affiliation: Licensed Social Worker; Saint Louis University, School of Social Service.

Major work:
> Tebb, S. (1995). *Coping successfully: Cognitive strategies for older caregivers.* New York: Garland Publishing.
> Author of other articles in the area of caregiving and social work education.

Population for whom the technique is appropriate: Adults caring for a person with a chronic disease/disability such as Alzheimer's disease, AIDS, or muscular dystrophy.

Cautionary notes: None.

Studies have shown that when one can successfully control daily aspects of one's environment, one's health and well-being improve. This scale was developed to assist clinicians with looking at areas where caregivers have control or can develop control in their life and thus increase their well-being.

The well-being scale (Figure 3.6) consisting of two subscales is a valid and reliable 45-item tool. The first subscale asks the caregivers to what extent they are satisfying their basic psychosocial needs. The second subscale asks caregivers to what degree they are managing activities of daily living in the physical, social, mental, and spiritual dimensions. Each item is responded to on a 5-point scale, from 1 = never or almost never to 5 = almost always. The scale is designed to be self-administered by the caregiver. It also can be completed by the clinician while interviewing the caregiver.

With its use, clinicians receive insight into what is happening on a daily basis with their clients, understand what care receivers were like before the chronic condition, pinpoint areas where the clients had control in their lives, discuss difficult topics with caregivers (e.g., sexual concerns), and determine where care-givers needed guidance and support. After completing the scale, the clinician and caregiver can view the results and examine what needs are being met² and how they are being met. The clinician can praise the caregiver for his or her efforts. The client and clinician can explore unmet activities and possible ways to meet these, such as exercising, relaxing, or beginning a new hobby. The clinician and caregiver then can consider how to best meet these needs and activities by using family, by using informal or formal support, and/or by learning new skills.

The use of this scale helps the clinician move away from the focus of pathology, deficits, disease, and problem assessment to an emphasis on fostering competencies, developing skills, and empowering those with whom he or she works. By focusing on the caregivers' regenerative capacity and resiliency, clinicians can support caregivers in developing and expanding their strengths and thus having a more positive experience in caregiving.

This scale also can be used with members of a support group. When administering the scale to members of a support group, the clinician asks those who are comfortable to share with the group one of their "1s" and one of their "5s" along with their ideas on why they scored the question as they did. After several members share, the clinician encourages all to share a "5." Suggestions from group members for how one might improve his or her well-being often come to mind when they share.

WELL-BEING SCALE

Basic Needs

Below are listed a number of basic needs. For each need listed, think about your life over the past three months. During this period of time, indicate to what extent you think each need has been met by circling the appropriate number on the scale provided below.

1 = Never or almost never
2 = Seldom, occasionally
3 = Sometimes
4 = Often, frequently
5 = Almost always

1. Having enough money	1 2 3 4 5
2. Eating a well-balanced diet	1 2 3 4 5
3. Getting enough sleep	1 2 3 4 5
4. Attending to your medical and dental needs	1 2 3 4 5
5. Having time for recreation	1 2 3 4 5
6. Feeling loved	1 2 3 4 5
7. Expressing love	1 2 3 4 5
8. Expressing laughter and joy	1 2 3 4 5
9. Expressing sadness	1 2 3 4 5
10. Enjoying sexual intimacy	1 2 3 4 5
11. Learning new skills	1 2 3 4 5
12. Feeling worthwhile	1 2 3 4 5
13. Feeling appreciated by others	1 2 3 4 5
14. Feeling good about family	1 2 3 4 5
15. Feeling good about yourself	1 2 3 4 5
16. Feeling secure about the future	1 2 3 4 5
17. Having close friendships	1 2 3 4 5
18. Having a home	1 2 3 4 5
19. Making plans about the future	1 2 3 4 5
20. Having people who think highly of you	1 2 3 4 5
21. Having meaning in your life	1 2 3 4 5
22. Expressing anger	1 2 3 4 5

Figure 3.6. Well-being Scale. Copyright © 1993 by Susan Tebb. Reproduce only with permission of the author, Susan Tebb, Saint Louis University.

Activities of Living

Below are listed a number of activities of living that each of us do or someone does for us. For each activity listed, think about your life over the past three months. During this period of time, indicate to what extent you think each activity of living has been met by circling the appropriate number on the scale provided below. You do not have to be the one doing the activity. You are being asked to rate the extent to which each activity of living has been taken care of in a timely way.

1 = Never or almost never
2 = Seldom, occasionally
3 = Sometimes
4 = Often, frequently
5 = Almost always

1. Buying food	1 2 3 4 5
2. Preparing meals	1 2 3 4 5
3. Getting the house clean	1 2 3 4 5
4. Getting the yard work done	1 2 3 4 5
5. Getting home maintenance done	1 2 3 4 5
6. Having adequate transportation	1 2 3 4 5
7. Purchasing clothing	1 2 3 4 5
8. Washing and caring for clothing	1 2 3 4 5
9. Relaxing	1 2 3 4 5
10. Exercising	1 2 3 4 5
11. Enjoying a hobby	1 2 3 4 5
12. Starting a new interest or hobby	1 2 3 4 5
13. Attending social events	1 2 3 4 5
14. Taking time for reflective thinking	1 2 3 4 5
15. Having time for inspirational or spiritual interests	1 2 3 4 5
16. Noticing the wonderment of things around you	1 2 3 4 5
17. Asking for support from your friends or family	1 2 3 4 5
18. Getting support from your friends or family	1 2 3 4 5
19. Laughing	1 2 3 4 5
20. Treating or rewarding yourself	1 2 3 4 5
21. Maintaining employment or career	1 2 3 4 5
22. Taking time for personal hygiene and appearance	1 2 3 4 5
23. Taking time to have fun with family or friends	1 2 3 4 5

Figure 3.6 (*Continued*).   Well-being Scale. Copyright © 1993 by Susan Tebb. Reproduce only with permission of the author, Susan Tebb, Saint Louis University.

POSTTRAUMATIC LOSS DEBRIEFING

Therapist: Rosemary A. Thompson, Ed.D., NCC, LPC

Affiliation: Licensed Professional Counselor; Public school administrator, Old Dominion University; Commonwealth Counseling & Consulting, Inc., Norfolk, Virginia.

Major works:
> Thompson, R. A. (1992). *School counseling renewal: Strategies for the twenty-first century.* Muncie, IN: Accelerated Development.
>
> Thompson, R. A. (1996). *Counseling techniques: Improving relationships with others, ourselves, our families, and our environment.* Bristol, PA: Taylor & Francis.
>
> Thompson, R. A. (in press.) *Nurturing an endangered generation: Empowering youth with critical social, emotional, and cognitive skills.* Bristol, PA: Taylor & Francis.

Population for whom the technique is appropriate: Clients who must deal with grief.

Cautionary notes: None.

Talking about a death and related anxieties in a secure environment provides a means to "work through" the experience and serves to prevent destructive fantasy building. Because loss is so painful emotionally, however, our natural tendency (personally or professionally) is to avoid or deny coming to terms with loss. Inherently, loss is a process that extends over time and more often than not has a lifelong impact.

Tasks of Mourning and Grief Counseling

- To accept the reality of the loss and to confront the fact that the person is dead; initial denial and avoidance becomes replaced by the realization of the loss.
- To experience the pain of grief. It is essential to acknowledge and work through this pain or it will manifest itself through self-defeating behavior(s).
- To adjust to an environment in which the deceased is missing. The survivor must face the loss of the many roles the deceased person filled in the survivor's life.

- To withdraw emotional energy and reinvest it in another relationship. An initial grief reaction to loss may be to make a pact with oneself never to love again. One must become open to new relationships and opportunities.
- To accept the pain of loss when dealing with the memory of the deceased.
- To overtly express sorrow, hostility, and guilt, and to be able to mourn openly.
- To understand the intense grief reactions associated with the loss; for example, to recognize that such symptoms as startle reactions— including restlessness, agitation, and anxiety—may temporarily interfere with one's ability to initiate and maintain normal patterns of activity.
- To come to terms with anger that often is generated toward the one who has died, toward self, or toward others; to redirect the sense of responsibility that somehow one should have prevented the death.

Strategies

The sudden, unexpected death by suicide or the sudden loss from an accidental death often produces a characteristic set of psychological and physiological responses among survivors. Persons exposed to traumatic events such as suicide or sudden loss often manifest the following stress reactions: irritability, sleep disturbances, anxiety, startle reactions, nausea, headaches, difficulty concentrating, confusion, fear, guilt, withdrawal, anger, and depression (Thompson, 1990, 1993).

Causes of Posttraumatic Stress Disorder (PTSD) can be grouped into three categories (a) natural disasters such as floods, fires, earthquakes, hurricanes, and tornados; (b) accidents such as a car crash, bombing, or shooting; and (c) human actions such as rape, robbery, assault, abduction, or abuse.

Diminished responsiveness to one's immediate environment with "psychic numbing" or "emotional anesthesia" usually begins soon after the traumatic event. Sometimes the stress reactions, however, appear immediately after the traumatic event or a delayed reaction may occur weeks or months later. With acute posttraumatic stress, the counseling intention is to help the client return as rapidly as possible to full activity, especially to the setting or circumstances in which the trauma occurred.

Goldenson (1984) provided the following profile of the stress disorder as an anxiety disorder produced by an uncommon, extremely stressful life event (e.g., assault, rape, military combat, flood, earthquake, hurricane, death camp, torture, car accident, or head trauma) and characterized by (a) reexperiencing the trauma in painful recollections or recurrent dreams or nightmares; (b) diminished responsiveness (emotional anesthesia or numbing) with disinterest in significant activities and with feelings of detachment and estrangement from others; and (c) such symptoms as heightened startle response, disturbed sleep, difficulty in concentrating or remembering, guilt about surviving when others did not, and avoidance of activities that call the traumatic event to mind (Goldenson, 1984, p. 573).

With chronic PTSD, anxiety and depression also are prevalent. The particular pattern of the emotional reaction and type of response will differ with each survivor depending on the relationship of the deceased, circumstances surrounding the death, and coping mechanisms of the survivors. Grinspoon (1991) provided 17 suggestions that counselors can utilize when dealing with a client who is experiencing PTSD:

- Provide a safe environment for confronting the traumatic event.
- Link events emotionally and intellectually to the symptoms.
- Restore identity and personality.
- Remain calm while listening to horrifying stories.
- Anticipate one's own feelings or responses and coping skills—dread, disgust, anger at clients or persons who had hurt them, guilt, and/or anxiety about providing enough help.
- Avoid overcommitment and detachment.
- Avoid identifying with the client or seeing oneself as rescuer.
- Tell the client that change may take some time.
- Introduce the subject of trauma to ask about terrifying experiences and about specific symptoms.
- Moderate extremes of reliving and denial while the client works through memories of trauma.
- Provide sympathy, encouragement, and reassurance.
- Try to limit external demands on the client.
- During periods of client numbing and withdrawal, pay more attention to the traumatic event itself.
- Help client bring memories to light by any means possible including dreams, association, fantasies, photographs, and old medical records. For children, utilize play therapy, dolls, coloring books, and drawings.
- Special techniques, systematic desensitization and implosion, can be used to eliminate conditioned fear of situations evoking memories and to achieve catharsis.
- Provide group therapy.

Posttraumatic Loss Debriefing (Thompson, 1990, 1993)

Posttraumatic loss debriefing is a structured approach to understanding and managing the physical and emotional responses of survivors and their loss experiences. It creates a supportive environment in which to process blocked communication that often interferes with the expression of grief or feelings of guilt, to correct distorted attitudes toward the deceased, and to discuss ways of coping with the loss. The purpose of the debriefing is to reduce the trauma associated with the sudden loss, initiate an adaptive grief process, and prevent further self-destructive or self-defeating behavior. The goals are accomplished by allowing for ventilation of feelings, allowing for exploration of symbols associated with the event, and enabling mutual support.

Posttraumatic loss debriefing is composed of six stages: introductory stage, fact stage, feeling stage, reaction stage, learning stage, and closure. Posttraumatic loss debriefing is a structured approach to the management of the acute emotional upset affecting one's ability to cope emotionally, cognitively, or behaviorally with the crisis situation. Successful resolution and psychological well-being are dependent upon interventions that prepare individuals for periods of stress and help survivors return to their pre-crisis equilibrium.

A debriefing should be organized 24 to 72 hours after the death. Natural feelings of denial and avoidance predominate during the first 24 hours. The debriefing can be offered to all persons affected by the loss. The tone must be positive, supportive, and understanding.

Counseling Intention. To process loss and grief; to inform about typical stress response and implications for participants.

Description.

1. **Introductory Stage:** Brief introductions to the debriefing process and establishment of rules for the process.
   - Define the nature, limits, roles, and goals within the debriefing process.
   - Clarify time limits, number of sessions, confidentiality, possibilities, and expectations to reduce unknowns and anxiety for survivors.
   - Encourage members to remain silent regarding details of the debriefing, especially details that could be associated with a particular individual.
   - Assure participants in a debriefing that the open discussion of their

feelings will, in no way, be utilized against them under any circumstances.

- Give reassurances that the caregiver-as-facilitator will continue to maintain an attitude of unconditional positive regard. Reduce the survivors initial anxieties to a level that permits them to begin talking.

2. **Fact Stage:** Warm-up and gathering information; recreating the event. During the fact phase, participants are asked to recreate the event for the facilitator. The focus of this stage is facts, not feelings.

- Encourage individuals to engage in a moderate level of self-disclosure statements such as, "I didn't know. . . . Could you tell me what that was for you?" This encourages self-disclosure.
- Try to achieve an accurate sensing of the survivor's world and communicate that understanding to him or her.
- Be aware of the survivor's choices of topics regarding the death to gain insight into his or her priorities for the moment.
- Help survivors see the many factors that contributed to the death to curtail self-blaming.
- Ask group members to make brief statements regarding their role, relationship with the deceased, how they heard about the death, and circumstances surrounding the event.
- Have group members take turns adding in details to make the incident come to life again.

This low initial interaction is a nonthreatening warm-up and naturally leads into a discussion of feelings in the next stage. It also provides a climate to share the details about the death and to intervene to prevent secrets or rumors that may divide survivors.

3. **Feeling Stage:** Expression of feelings surrounding the event and exploration of symbols. At this stage, survivors should have the opportunity to share the burden of the feelings that they are experiencing and to be able to do so in an nonjudgmental, supportive, and understanding manner. Survivors must be permitted to talk about themselves, identify and express feelings, identify their own behavioral reactions, and relate to the immediate present (i.e., the "here and now").

- Communicate acceptance and understanding of a survivor's feelings. Acceptance of the person's feelings often helps him or her feel better immediately. It also can serve as a developmental transition to a healthier coping style in the future. Thoughtful clarification or reflection of feelings can lead to growth and change, rather than self-depreciation and self-pity.
- Offer each person in the group an opportunity to answer these and

a variety of other questions regarding feelings. Often survivors will confront the emotion of anger and where the feeling is directed. It is important that survivors express thoughts of responsibility regarding the event and process the accompanying feelings of sadness.

- Take care to assure that no one gets left out of the discussion and that no one dominates the discussion at the expense of others.

At times, the facilitator has to do very little. Survivors have a tendency to start talking, and the whole process goes along with only limited guidance from the facilitator. People most often will discuss their fears, anxieties, concerns and feelings of guilt, frustration, anger, and ambivalence. All of their feelings—positive or negative, big or small—are important and need to be listened to and expressed. More importantly, however, this process allows survivors to see that subtle changes are occurring between what happened then and what is happening now.

4. **Reaction Phase:** Explanation of cognitive and physical reactions and ramifications of the stress response. This stage explores the physical and cognitive reactions to the traumatic event. Acute reactions can last from a few days to a few weeks. Inherently, the survivor wants to move toward some form of resolution and articulates that need in terms such as, "I can't go on like this anymore," "Something has got to give," "Please help me shake this feeling," or "I feel like I'm losing my mind." Typical anxiety reactions are a sense of dread, fear of losing control, or the inability to focus or concentrate.
   - Ask questions such as, "What reactions did you experience at the time of the incident or when you were informed of the death?" and "What are you experiencing now?"
   - Encourage survivors to discuss what is going on with them in their peer, school, work, and family relationships.
   - To help clarify reactions, provide a model for describing reactions, such as the following: "ownership + feeling word + description of behavior." For example, "I am afraid to go to sleep at night since this has happened," or "I feel guilty about not seeing the signs that he was considering suicide."

5. **Learning Stage:** Understanding posttraumatic stress reactions to loss. This stage is designed to assist survivors in learning new coping skills to deal with their grief reactions. It is also therapeutic to help survivors realize that others are having similar feelings and experiences.
   - Assume the responsibility of teaching the group something about their typical stress response reactions.
   - Describe how typical and natural it is for people to experience a

wide variety of feelings, emotions, and physical reactions to any traumatic event. It is not unique but a universal shared reaction.
- Be alert to danger signals in order to prevent negative destructive outcomes from a crisis experience and to help survivors return to their pre-crisis equilibrium and interpersonal stability.

This stage also serves as a primary prevention component for future self-defeating or self-destructive behaviors by identifying the normal responses to a traumatic event in a secure, therapeutic, environment with a caring, trusted facilitator.

6. **Closure:** Wrap-up of loose ends; questions and answers; final reassurances; and action planning, referrals, and follow-up. Human crises that involve posttraumatic stress often, if debriefed appropriately, serve as catalysts for personal growth. This final stage seeks to wrap up loose ends and answer outstanding questions.

Phases of Recovery

Further, Petersen and Straub (1992) classified the recovery process into four phases.

The Emergency or Outcry Phase. The survivor experiences heightened "fight or flight" reactions to the life-threatening event. This phase lasts as long as the survivor believes it to last. Pulse, blood pressure, respiration, and muscle activity all are increased. Concomitant feelings of fear and helplessness predominate. Termination of the event itself is followed by relief and confusion. Preoccupation centers around questions about why the event happened and the long-term consequences.

The Emotional Numbing and Denial Phase. The survivor shelters psychic well-being by burying the traumatic experience in subconscious memory. By avoiding the experience, the victim temporarily reduces anxiety and stress responses. Many survivors may remain at this stage unless they receive professional intervention.

The Intrusive-repetitive Phase. The survivor has nightmares, mood swings, intrusive images, and startle reactions. Overreliance on defense mechanisms (e.g., intellectualization, projection, or denial) or self-defeating behaviors (e.g., alcohol or other drugs) may be integrated into coping behaviors in an effort to repress the traumatic event. At this juncture, the delayed stress becomes so overwhelming that the survivor may seek help or become so mired in the pathology of the situation that professional intervention becomes necessary.

The Reflective-transition Phase. The survivor is able to put the traumatic event into perspective. He or she begins to interact positively and constructively with a future orientation and exhibits a willingness to put the traumatic event behind him or her. (pp. 246-247)

References

Goldenson, R. M. (1984). Post-traumatic stress disorder. *Longman Dictionary of Psychology and Psychiatry*. New York: Longman.

Grinspoon, L. (Ed.). (1991, March). Post-traumatic stress: Part II. *Harvard Mental Health Letter, 7*(9), 1-4.

Peterson, S., & Straub, R. (1992). *School crisis survival guide*. West Nyack, NY: Center for Applied Research in Education.

Thompson, R. A. (1990). Post-traumatic loss debriefing: Providing immediate support for survivors of suicide or sudden loss. *Highlights: An ERIC/CAPS Digest*. Ann Arbor, MI: Counseling and Personnel Services Clearinghouse.

Thompson, R. A. (1993). Post-traumatic stress and post-traumatic loss debriefing: Brief strategic intervention for survivors of sudden loss. *The School Counselor, 36*(1), 22-27.

DRAW YOUR FAMILY TABLE/FAMILY-O-GRAM

Therapist: James P. Trotzer, Ph.D.

Affiliation: Certified psychologist; Fellow, Association for Specialists in Group Work; private practice; adjunct professor of Counselor Education, Johns Hopkins University, Baltimore, Maryland.

Major works:
> Trotzer, J. P. (1989). *The counselor and the group* (2nd ed.). Muncie, IN: Accelerated Development.
>
> Trotzer, J. P., & Trotzer, T. (1986). *Marriage and family: Better ready than not.* Muncie, IN: Accelerated Development.

Population for whom the technique is appropriate: This group technique is particularly useful in groups where members are examining the impact of their family of origin and/or current family dynamics on their personality and interpersonal dynamics. Age range of applicability is school age through adult. It is also useful in training with counselors and caregivers when you want to emphasize the impact of a system's dynamics and assist helpers in learning to think systematically.

Cautionary notes: This technique can have a powerful impact on participants, particularly if the death directive is included in the process. As such, make certain that there is sufficient processing time for members to deal with their feelings and reactions. In addition, the group verbalization effect also tends to be quite overwhelming in the family-o-gram, and sufficient attention must be given to debriefing the members much like the sharing phase in a psychodrama. Both the volunteer and the participants need time to share their reactions.

Family Table

> Give the clients in the group the following instructions (points 1 through 4):
>
> 1. On a large sheet of paper, draw the shape of the table your family ate at when you were growing up. (Select a time frame when you were between the ages of 7 and 18, or use your current family.)
> 2. Place members of your family around the table in their usual places using squares to represent males and circles to represent females. Identify each person by name or role (e.g., mother, father, grandfather, etc.).

3. Near each family member at the table, write a least two descriptive phrases or comments that portray each family member's personality.

4. On the surface of the table, write descriptors (words or phrases) that describe the atmosphere of the family and what it was like living with the family.

5. Sharing: Have each group member share his or her childhood table with the group.

6. (Optional for training purposes) After sharing, have each member pass his or her table to the person on his or her right. Instruct that person to arbitrarily cross out one member of the family by placing an *x* over that person. Return the table to the original member. Next have each member describe how his or her family would be today (in the present) and how he or she would be different if the person who was crossed out had died at the point in time when the family table was depicted.

Family-O-Gram

After each person has shared his or her table, ask for a volunteer to participate in an exercise to examine the communication dynamics in the family. Using the volunteer's table, proceed as follows:

1. Have the volunteer select a group member to represent each person at the table including the volunteer himself or herself. Have the volunteer give a verbal description of each family member as he or she is selected and specify a *typical statement that family member would make.* Each family member is to remember the statement and present it in the character of the family member described.

2. Once the descriptions and statements have been assigned, place the volunteer in the center and form the other members around him or her in the manner depicted by the family table.

3. Starting with a parent figure (usually father), have the volunteer face the person and make eye contact. When the volunteer does this, the family member must make the statement in character. The volunteer then rotates to the next person on the right, repeating the procedure until each family member has given his or her statement to the volunteer in the center. Repeat the rotation at least three times without interruption.

4. After three rotations, have the family members move in closer to the volunteer in the center. Instruct the volunteer to close his or her eyes, and then have all the family members make their statements at once,

trying to get the attention of the volunteer in the center. After 15 to 20 seconds, stop the procedure and process the experience with the volunteer whose table was utilized.

5. Processing this technique should occur after the sharing of the table, following the death directive if it is used, and upon completion of the family-o-gram.

THE TECHNIQUE OF NUCLEUS THERAPY

Therapist: Ellen Walkenstein, M.D.

Affiliation: Board Certified Psychiatrist, private practice, Wyncote, Pennsylvania; member, Board of Directors, Center for the Study of Psychiatry, Bethesda, Maryland.

Major works:
Walkenstein, E. (1972). *Beyond the couch.* New York: Crown Publishers.
Walkenstein, E. (1982). *Fat chance.* New York: Pilgrim Press.
Walkenstein, E. (1983). *Your inner therapist.* Philadelphia, PA: Westminster Press.
Author of numerous articles, television appearances (e.g., Sally Jessy Raphael Show), and conductor of workshops in the U.S. and Europe (e.g., London, Paris, Rome, Florence, and Naples).

Population for whom the technique is intended: Appropriate for young and old, individual and group treatment, addicted or food-obsessed.

Cautionary note: Although this is a step-by-step educational process of confronting the self-in-hiding, it involves a discovering rather than being taught.

Throughout my eclectic psychiatric practice, I have used myriads of techniques that many others have used with one glaring exception: I never have found it necessary to prescribe ECT or drugs. From the beginning, using an amalgamation of Freudian and Reichian concepts, and later Gestalt, behavior, and cognitive strategies, I tended toward intensive interpersonal involvement. In my hospital work with psychotic patients, I would see them daily and as soon as appropriate would bring relevant family members to our sessions.

In the mid-1970s, I developed what I called the Nucleus Concept, which for me, my patients, and students, illuminated the causative factors in the neuroses and psychoses. I believed I finally had found the fundamental framework for which I had been searching all those years. While I continue to use a multitude of "techniques," the leitmotif that runs through my therapy today is the Nucleus. I first mentioned this entity in my book *Fat Chance* (1982), which portrays people with eating disorders. A complete, detailed description of the Nucleus and its effects will be depicted in two of my forthcoming books: *Mom's Alive and Well and Living Inside Me* and *The Nucleus Concept: Pursuit of the*

Unicorn. Since these two books have not yet been published, I am pleased to present the concept here for the first time in print.

And now, the Nucleus Concept. The presence of the Nucleus starts in infancy. As infants, we absorb and imitate everything. We are totally, nonselectively permeable. Everything comes in. Especially everything about the person who is the most with us at the beginning—our primary caretaker. When we reflect (imitate) our mother's (or other's) good and desirable qualities, she smiles, cuddles, and coos with pleasure. But when we reflect back her undesirable traits, the traits she cannot stand to see or acknowledge in herself, we may get a frown, a yell, or a broken bone.

So, very early in life we learn to hide the qualities of mother that she does not want to acknowledge in herself. We conceal these traits so well that we succeed in blinding ourselves to their presence in us. These hidden traits become our deepest secret and the source of our most intense shame. A person can go for a lifetime in denial, enduring disturbed relationships and disturbing symptoms. These distracting disturbances serve the person both to conceal and at the same time to keep connected with the original caretaker and her or his traits. The nucleus accounts for our repetitive choice of assaultive and undesirable mates as a way of concealing, denying, and connecting with our Nucleus traits. The term "nucleus" evolved in the early course of my work with the concept as I became aware that the mother (or early caretaker) and her traits are imbedded firmly in us like the nucleus of a cell and, like the cell's nucleus, our parental Nucleus dominates and dictates our behavior and relationships.

In Nucleus Therapy, as these revelations are brought to awareness, working through despairs, rages, lovings, and hatings, the energies used up in the person's attempts in the camouflaging are released. They then are made available to the individual who can use the energies for more constructive relationships with the self and others.

Using James Baldwin's "we cannot change what we do not know" as a starting-off point, it becomes clear in Nucleus work that change requires knowledge of our deceptions and cover-ups. The release from symptoms and from the compulsion to repeat destructive relationships are the happy result.

Among the useful techniques used in uncovering the Nucleus are the homework assignments wherein the person lists traits of the mother that caused the most despair, anger, and pain. Role-playing in the session is useful if the person is willing to play the role of the parent exhibiting these traits. This often reevokes the person's reactions as a child to this mother—the shames, hurts, tears, longings.

Another useful homework task is for the person to list the major traits of the mate one has chosen. The similarity of the mate (male or female) with one's mother often comes as a startling, revelatory experience.

The ultimate and most excruciating step of all is the recognition that those hurtful traits are alive and well inside the person. When this last step is undertaken, not through didactic explanations but as a kind of self-achieved awesome epiphany, the person is already "home free." The connection with the real self and all of its imprintings becomes the true goal of the therapeutic journey.

Finally, I believe that more important than all the techniques and concepts of therapy, no matter how brilliant, is the degree of empathy, caring, and simple humanity of the therapist.

BIBLIOTHERAPY

Therapist: Bea Wehrly, Ph.D.

Affiliation: Counselor Educator Emeritus, Western Illinois University, Macomb, Illinois; author.

Major works:
> Wehrly, B. (1995). *Pathways to multicultural counseling competence: A developmental journey.* Pacific Grove, CA: Brooks/Cole.
> Wehrly, B. (1996). *Counseling interracial individuals and families.* Alexandria, VA: American Counseling Association.

Population for whom the technique is appropriate: Bibliotherapy can be used with people of all ages and with clients with a great variety of problems or issues. I found it is especially effective in group work with elementary-age children.

Cautionary notes: Bibliotherapy is difficult to use with people with developmentally-delayed cognitive development. Individuals who have difficulty with abstract thinking probably will profit little from the use of bibliotherapy. Counselors who have worked with cognitively handicapped individuals may be able to simplify the process so that these clients could profit from the use of stories for therapeutic purposes.

Special planning is needed for use of bibliotherapy with individuals who are sight- or hearing-impaired. There are now many talking books (books on tape) on the market as well as books in Braille that can be used for bibliotherapy. The selection of books may be more limited, however, than for people with normal eyesight and hearing.

Bibliotherapy is the use of books or stories for therapeutic purposes. Bibliotherapy can be experienced through hearing, reading, or seeing a story acted out on the stage or in a video or movie.

Some general guidelines or assumptions that undergird the use of bibliotherapy are (a) a problem exists now or in the future for the reader or listener; (b) the reader or listener identifies with a character and situation in the story; and (c) through becoming personally involved with the character and situation in the story, the reader or listener gains insight for solving present or future problematic issues (Cornett & Cornett, 1980; Wehrly, 1995, 1996).

There are three stages in the process of bibliotherapy: identification, catharsis, and insight (Cornett & Cornett, 1980). In order for the readers or listeners to experience all of these processes, they must be able to identify with a character in the story. Through identifying with this story character, the readers or listeners experience catharsis, a purge of emotions, and realize that others face and find solutions to similar problems. Following identification, they are able to develop insight and consider possible solutions for their present and future problems.

Cornett and Cornett (1980) suggested four benefits that the reader or listener may receive from the use of bibliotherapy as a therapeutic tool.

1. The experience is a vicarious one since the situation is happening to someone else. This makes it safe since someone else is experiencing the problem. There is little threat to the reader, listener, or viewer.
2. The persons participating in bibliotherapy realize that others, also, face problems similar to theirs, so they feel less alone.
3. Through following the ways that the lead characters in the stories work out their problems, the participants learn that most problems have several possible solutions. This helps readers or listeners consider alternatives rather than limit problem-solving to one right or wrong choice.
4. Through considering a variety of alternatives for problem solution, participants learn to engage in critical thinking.

Bibliotherapy is used in an age-appropriate and situation-specific manner (Wehrly, 1996). The vocabulary level must be appropriate to the cognitive developmental level of the individual, or individuals, with whom it is used. Stories used must include issue- or problem-content with which the listener or reader can identify, and the stories must be reality based. Fairy tales are not appropriate for bibliotherapy.

Establishing a relationship with the client (or clients, if the counselor is working with a group) is a necessary prerequisite to the use of bibliotherapeutic techniques. The counselor must have become acquainted with the issues that the client (or clients) brings to counseling.

The counselor then goes to a variety of annotated sources that list books on a wide range of topics. I suggest the following annotated sources for choosing books for bibliotherapy with children or adolescents: the first five volumes of *The Bookfinder* (Dreyer, 1977, 1981, 1985, 1989, 1994); *Our Family, Our Friends, Our World: An Annotated Guide to Significant Multicultural Books for Children and Teenagers* (Miller-Lachmann, 1992); *Against Borders: Promoting Books for a Multicultural World* (Rochman, 1993); and *Dealing with Diversity through Multicultural Fiction: Library-Classroom Partnerships* (Johnson & Smith, 1993). If the counselor is working individually with a child or adolescent who will read his or her own story, it is a good idea to have two or three books from which the client can choose.

The bibliotherapeutic process includes the reading of, or listening to, the story. When using the process with a group of children, I have found it helpful to tape record the story and play the tape to the group. This gave me the opportunity to watch the nonverbal reactions of individuals in the group and stop the tape for frequent discussion of the story. Open-ended questions are helpful in eliciting children's perceptions of what is happening in the story. Some of the follow-up activities that might be used are the following: discussing various alternatives that lead characters had in working out their problems; writing, telling, or acting out a different ending to the story; and making pictures related to the story. Taking time to process is important since it cannot be assumed that individuals will automatically gain insight on problem solving from being exposed to the story.

My experience in using this technique with groups of children as young as seven or eight years of age is that they get into the story very quickly and often are talking about problems that they have that are similar even before the story is finished. Presenting this as a group process has the advantage of group members "piggy backing" off each other's ideas and helping their peers consider more than one alternative.

References

Cornett, C. E., & Cornett, C. F. (1980). *Bibliotherapy: The right book at the right time.* Bloomington, IN: Phi Delta Kappa.

Dreyer, S. S. (1977). *The bookfinder.* Circle Pines, MN: American Guidance Services.

Dreyer, S. S. (1981). *The bookfinder* (vol. 2). Circle Pines, MN: American Guidance Services.

Dreyer, S. S. (1985). *The bookfinder 3: When kids need books.* Circle Pines, MN: American Guidance Services.

Dreyer, S. S. (1989). *The bookfinder 4: When kids need books.* Circle Pines, MN: American Guidance Services.

Dreyer, S. S. (1994). *The bookfinder* (vol. 5). Circle Pines, MN: American Guidance Services.

Johnson, L., & Smith, S. (1993). *Dealing with diversity through multicultural fiction: Library-classroom partnerships.* Chicago: American Library Association.

Miller-Lachmann, L. (1992). *Our family, our friends, our world: An annotated guide to significant multicultural books for children and teenagers.* New Providence, NJ: Bowker.

Rochman, H. (1993). *Against borders: Promoting books for a multicultural world.* Chicago: American Library Association.

Wehrly, B. (1995). *Pathways to multicultural counseling competence: A developmental journey.* Pacific Grove, CA: Brooks/Cole.

Wehrly, B. (1996). *Counseling interracial individuals and families.* Alexandria, VA: American Counseling Association.

THE "TELEPHONE" TECHNIQUE

Therapist: William J. Weikel, Ph.D.

Affiliation: National Certified Counselor; Certified Clinical Mental Health Counselor; Diplomate, American Board of Vocational Experts; professor and chair, Department of Leadership, Morehead State University, Morehead Kentucky; owner, Eastern Kentucky Counseling and Rehabilitation Services.

Major works:
> Hughes, P. R., & Weikel, W. J. (1993). *The counselor as expert witness.* Laurel, MD: American Correctional Association.
> Palmo, A. J., & Weikel, W. J. (1996). *Foundations of mental health counseling.* Springfield, IL: Charles C. Thomas.
> Author or co-author of 35 refereed journal articles.

Population for whom the technique is appropriate: For use with older adolescents through adult populations, primarily in group but also individual counseling.

Cautionary notes: Counselors and therapists using this technique should be well-grounded in group processes and familiar with the Gestalt approach.

The telephone technique borrows from Gestalt counseling theory in helping clients bring situations that may be "there and then" to the present or "here and now." It is similar in some ways to the empty chair technique used by Perls and others in that it allows clients to develop conversations with others not present in group and to deal with unfinished business they may have with that person or persons.

I frequently use this technique with college students who have unresolved issues with a parent who may be in another town or even deceased. The client, after discussing an issue that remains unresolved and is troublesome for him or her is given a telephone that is not wired or is asked to use an imaginary telephone to call the person with whom the client has unresolved feelings. With help from the therapist and/or other group members, a dialogue begins. The client can put the other party "on hold" to gain advice or direction from the group in order to role-play a conversation or try alternative approaches. By using the telephone technique, the client can confront in a less threatening manner those persons with whom he or she has unfinished business or unresolved feelings. It is an excellent way to bring about closure, even with deceased persons.

I have found that frequently after completing this process, the client actually will initiate a phone call with the other party and bring about "in vivo" closure to a situation that has been troubling for some time. By using this technique in the safety of the group setting and in a role-play situation, clients gain the practice and confidence to deal with interpersonal (and sometimes intrapsychic) situations that many have long avoided.

BODY SCAN

Therapist: Ira David Welch, Ed.D., ABPP

Affiliation: Licensed psychologist; Director of Training, Counseling Psychology, University of Northern Colorado, Greeley, Colorado.

Major works:
> Welch, I. D., Medeiros, D. C., & Tate, G. A. (1982). *Beyond burnout.* Englewood Cliffs, NJ: Prentice-Hall.
>
> Welch, I. D., Tate, G. A., & Medeiros, D. C. (1987). *Self-actualization: An annotated bibliography of theory and research.* New York: Garland Publishing.
>
> Welch, I. D., Zawistoski, R. F., & Smart, D. W. (1991). *Encountering death: Structured activities for death awareness.* Muncie, IN: Accelerated Development.

Population for whom the technique is appropriate: Adolescents and adults.

Cautionary notes: While there is no group for whom this technique is contraindicated, it seems best suited for adolescents and adults.

This is an exploratory technique designed to assist the client in discussing some issue in his or her life when he or she cannot seem to identify the emotion that accompanies the issue. It is a form of body work.

The therapist identifies the issue with the client (e.g., "I can't talk to my wife."). Then, the therapist might say, "I want you to do something. I'll describe it for you, and then I want you to use your hand as a scanner for feeling in your body. You know how a computer might scan a photograph for a particular image or object? I want you to scan your body for feelings about this issue. Close your eyes and move your hand from the top of your head across your body down to your feet. When you feel something, a catch or any feeling, stop and then move on. Do you have any questions? Do it now."

The therapist observes the scan and notes any stops. When the scan is completed, ask the client to touch the places when the scan stopped. Have the client label that part of the body touched (e.g., head, chest, stomach, knee). After the client has identified and labeled the area of the body touched, have the client give his or her symbolic understanding of that part of the body. There are common places clients touch, and each has a somewhat literal interpretation of the meaning. For example:

Head= intellectual/cognitive (The client may feel stupid about the situation.);

Shoulders= heavy load (The client is carrying a burden.);

Mouth/Throat= communication (The client may not feel comfortable talking about the issue.);

Throat= choking (The client may feel suffocated by the issue.);

Heart= love (The client may feel unloved.);

Chest= armor, box (The client may feel defensive, trapped, or that something is hidden from him or her.);

Stomach= nurturance, guts (The client may feel unloved and may lack the courage to face the issue.);

Genitals= sexual (The issue might be infidelity; he or she is being "screwed.");

Back= pain (The issue or person is a pain.);

Knee= kneeling (The issue may be one of submission; the client may feel like a "slave."); and

Feet= running (The client wants to get out of the situation.).

The method of interpretation here is to be as literal as can be. Consider the first impression that comes to mind, or a common cliché. It is important to have the client identify the part of the body touched and the symbolic meaning given to that part of the body. Then, the therapist can add anything that seems significant to the therapist. This technique is a quick way to identify the emotion attributed to an issue in the life of a client. While the description is long, the actual time needed to complete this technique is short and is meant to quickly provide an insight for the client and therapist.

RATIONAL-EMOTIVE IMAGERY (REI)

Therapist: Jerry Wilde, Ph.D.

Affiliation: Psychologist, Ottawa University, Kansas; private practice.

Major works:
> Wilde, J. (1992). *Rational counseling with school aged populations: A practical guide.* Muncie, IN: Accelerated Development.
> Wilde, J. (1994). *Anger management in schools: Alternatives to student violence.* Lancaster, PA: Technomic Publishing.
> Wilde, J. (1995). *Why kids struggle in school: A guide to overcoming underachievement.* Salt Lake City, UT: Northwest Publishing.

Population for whom the technique is appropriate: Adolescents and adults with anger and anxiety problems.

Cautionary notes: This technique is not recommended for severely depressed clients.

The following is an example of how REI is used with clients who have anger problems. Start by telling clients to get as relaxed as possible in their chair with both feet on the floor.

> **Therapist:** *Amy, I want you to listen very closely to what I'm going to tell you. I want you to be aware only of my voice and focus on what I say. Try to block everything else out of your mind for the time being.*

> **Therapist:** *Close your eyes and take a deep breath. As you breathe out, notice that you are becoming more relaxed. Each time you breathe out you are getting more relaxed and more focused on my voice.* (Author's note: This can be expanded to meet the needs of your client. It may take several minutes to get a particular client to relax and others may take very little time.)

> **Therapist:** *Imagine you are back in your room two nights ago and you were feeling very angry about your parents' upcoming divorce. Picture your room in your mind. See all the posters on the walls and everything else that is in the room. Now go ahead and let yourself feel like you did that night. Feel all the anger you felt back then. Stay*

with that scene and try to feel just like you felt two nights ago. When you feel that way, wiggle your finger and let me know if you're there. (Author's note: It is a good idea to look for behavioral signs confirming that clients are actually feeling angry. Their jaws will tighten, their brows furrow, and some even make fists.)

Therapist: *Stay with that feeling. Keep imagining that you are in your bedroom.* (Author's note: Allow the client to stay in this state for approximately 20 to 40 seconds. Remind him or her to mentally stay in the situation and to remain upset.)

Therapist: *Now I want you to calm yourself down. Stay in the bedroom in your mind, but try to calm down. Instead of being very upset, try to get calmer. Instead of being enraged, try to work toward only feeling irritated. Keep working at it until you can calm yourself down. When you can make yourself calm, wiggle your finger again.*

Usually clients can reach a state of relative calm within a short time. Once they have wiggled their finger, it is time to bring the clients back to the here and now of your office. The first question to ask is, "What did you say to yourself to calm yourself down?" If the client was able to calm himself or herself, then he or she had to be thinking rationally. The only other way to calm oneself would be to mentally leave the situation (i.e., no longer visualize the bedroom or change the situation in some way). This usually does not happen, but if it does, try the exercise over encouraging the client to keep imagining the scene but working to calm down.

Clients then will be able to record the thought that allowed them to calm down and use this thought in their homework. A typical calming thought that might have been produced from the above scenario would be, "Even though I don't like the thought of my parents divorcing, I can live with it. I don't have to approve of their actions."

Once the client has produced a calming thought, he or she can practice this mental imagery several times a day. The more the client practices, the better he or she will be at overcoming his or her anger or anxiety obstacle. Usually clients can learn to do REI by themselves after having been lead through it a couple of times by the therapist. It is also possible to make a recording of REI for the client to use in the privacy of his or her own home. Some clients like using the tape rather than leading themselves through REI. Both methods can and will be effective if used regularly.

REI also is well-suited to be used with anxious clients as it allows clients to experience the feared event mentally, even in the safety of their home or your office. If the images become too much for them, clients are aware that this is only an exercise. They are in complete control and can leave the scene in their mind. That is the beauty of REI—it allows clients to practice dealing with their difficulties or issues in a safe environment yet benefits them significantly in their attempts to overcome the problem.

Positive effects from REI can be almost immediate. Armed with this knowledge, the client has a powerful tool to use nearly anytime, anywhere, to help themselves overcome a wide range of problems. It really is this simple, and it really works that well.

CLIENT INNER SELF-EVALUATION:
A NECESSARY PRELUDE TO CHANGE

Therapist: Robert E. Wubbolding, Ed.D.

Affiliation: Licensed counselor; psychologist; professor of counseling at Xavier University; Director of the Center for Reality Therapy, Cincinnati, Ohio.

Major works:
> Wubbolding, R. (1988). *Using reality therapy.* New York: HarperCollins.
> Wubbolding, R. (1991). *Understanding reality therapy.* New York: Harper-Collins.
> Wubbolding, R. (in press). *Reality therapy with children.*

Population for whom the technique is appropriate: All clients.

Cautionary notes: The cautionary notes are the same as applied to any theory and method following the standard practices as reflected in codes of ethics.

Many counseling systems incorporate homework, assignments, and active planning into their delivery systems. Counselors and therapists often elicit, suggest, and even require that clients practice skills and implement behaviors outside counseling sessions. Sometimes these attempts are successful, and often they are not. If true change is to take place, clients need to come to the belief and make a judgment that the way they are living is not as effective as it could be. Hence, therapists can expand their arsenal of skills and facilitate more rapid and effective change by assisting clients to self-evaluate (Glasser, 1985; Wubbolding, 1988, 1991).

Importance of Self-evaluation

As human beings, we have inside of us a characteristic I often have called, "an undying belief in behaviors that do not work." We repeatedly search for lost items in the same place, we shout at our children, we procrastinate easily performed tasks, etc. Accompanying these choices is the implicit inner statement, "If it isn't working, keep doing it." In the counseling technique of self-evaluation, the helper holds a metaphorical mirror before clients and asks them to evaluate themselves, to examine the effectiveness of their lives. This is done in an explicit and precise manner. To be effective, self-evaluation cannot be presumed. Counselors using this tool do not assume that because people seek counseling they have evaluated that they want to make specific change. Many people desire an outcome but do not see that their behavior is ineffective.

Specific Modes of Self-evaluation

Use of this technique will elicit several kinds of inner judgment from clients.

1. "Is the overall direction of your life a plus or a minus?" "Are you headed in the direction you would like to go?"
2. "Are your specific actions effective in getting what you want?" "When you did such and such yesterday, did it help or hurt you?" "Did it help or hurt the people around you?"
3. "Did such and such a behavior violate the rules?" (This question is useful for students who believe that antisocial actions help them.)
4. "Is what you did or are doing acceptable?" "Is it in line with or against any unwritten rules?"
5. "Is what you want from others, from yourself, from school, from work, and from society realistically attainable?"
6. "Is what you want genuinely good for you?" "Will it help you or hurt you in the long run and in the short run if you have what you want?"
7. "Does it help you view the world—parents, students, friends, employees, etc.—in the manner you have chose?"
8. "Are the plans you have made for change genuinely satisfying to you, and are they helpful in attaining your wants (goals that have been evaluated previously)?" "Does your plan fulfill the characteristics of an effective plan? Is it simple, attainable, measurable, immediate and controlled (SAMIC) by you, the planner?"

The above formulations are intended to be useable. Still they need to be adapted to specific situations, to the age, and to the developmental stage of the clients.

Conclusion

These eight forms of inner self-evaluation are like a mirror held before clients. They conduct a personal inventory on the effectiveness of clients' choices, thinking, and perceptions. Clients can opt for change more readily after they have decided that their current choices are not helping them.

References

Glasser, W. (1985). *Control theory.* New York: HarperCollins.

Wubbolding, R. (1988). *Using reality therapy.* New York: HarperCollins.

Wubbolding, R. (1991). *Understanding reality therapy.* New York: HarperCollins.

Part IV

15 RECOMMENDATIONS FOR EFFECTIVELY IMPLEMENTING COUNSELING AND THERAPY TECHNIQUES

1. Use only techniques with which you feel comfortable.
2. Carry out the strategy with a spirit of empathy and optimism.
3. Always check ethical guidelines prior to implementing any technique.
4. Use caution to ensure that clients are not embarrassed. This is especially pertinent in couples counseling, marriage and family therapy, and group work.
5. If you are a student or are undergoing supervision for licensing or certification, check with your supervisor prior to implementation.
6. Consider role-playing any technique with a trained colleague or supervisor before you actually attempt it for the first time with a client.
7. Never attempt a technique for which you have no training.
8. Do not assume that even a powerful technique will work in every case.
9. Do not assume that a technique that worked well with a client will work effectively with the same client at a later date.
10. Always take multicultural and diversity considerations into account.
11. Use only verbiage the client can understand.
12. Bend, fold, and mutilate existing strategies to increase your comfort level and to meet the needs of your clients.
13. Realize that certain techniques must be used repeatedly in order to be effective.
14. Realize that therapeutic timing can make or break a technique.
15. Process the impact of the technique with the client when appropriate.

ABOUT THE EDITOR

Howard G. Rosenthal, Ed.D., is the author of the *Encyclopedia of Counseling* and the popular *NBCC and State Counselor Examination* audio series. Therapists nationwide use his materials to prepare for licensure and certification exams. He also wrote the innovative book, *Not with My Life I Don't: Preventing Your Suicide and That of Others* and the companion tapes, *Suicide Prevention for Young People* and *Suicide Prevention: Crash Course for Counselors and Therapists.* His text, *Help Yourself to Positive Mental Health,* co-authored by Joseph Hollis, is a popular bibliotherapeutic work.

He is listed in the National Directory of Distinguished Providers for Counseling and Development, Who's Who Among Human Services Professionals, Who's Who in the Midwest, and Who's Who Among America's Teachers. In 1988, he was inducted into the St. Louis Community College Hall of Fame for his accomplishments.

Dr. Rosenthal received his master's degree from the University of Missouri at St. Louis and his doctorate from St. Louis University. Over 100,000 people have heard his mental health lectures making him one of the most popular speakers in the Midwest. He has been a consultant and a guest on numerous radio and television shows. He has appeared as the expert in videos and movies and has been quoted frequently in magazine and newspaper articles.

He currently has a private practice in St. Charles, Missouri, is Director of the Human Services Program at St. Louis Community College at Florissant Valley, and teaches graduate courses at Webster University.